Instructor's Manual
Interactions 1
Reading

4th Edition

Prepared by
Janet Podnecky

McGraw-Hill
Contemporary

McGraw-Hill/Contemporary

A Division of The McGraw-Hill Companies

Interactions 1 Reading Instructor's Manual, 4th Edition

Published by McGraw-Hill/Contemporary, a business unit of The McGraw-Hill Companies, Inc., 1221 Avenue of the Americas, New York, NY 10020. Copyright © 2002, 1996, 1990, 1985 by The McGraw-Hill Companies, Inc. All rights reserved. No part of this publication may be reproduced or distributed in any form or by any means, or stored in a database or retrieval system, without the prior written consent of The McGraw-Hill Companies, Inc., including, but not limited to, in any network or other electronic storage or transmission, or broadcast for distance learning.

 This book is printed on recycled, acid-free paper containing 10% postconsumer waste.

2 3 4 5 6 7 8 9 0 PBT/PBT 0 9 8 7 6 5 4 3 2

ISBN 0-07-248140-4

Editorial director: *Tina B. Carver*
Series editor: *Annie Sullivan*
Development editors: *Louis Carrillo, Annie Sullivan*
Director of marketing: *Thomas P. Dare*
Production and composition: *A Good Thing, Inc.*
Printer: *Phoenix Color*

www.mhcontemporary.com/interactionsmosaic

TABLE OF CONTENTS

Introduction   iv

General Teaching Suggestions   iv

Administering the Reading Placement Test   vi

Using the Chapter Quizzes   vi

Teaching Notes

     Chapter 1 School Life Around the World   1

     Chapter 2 Experiencing Nature   8

     Chapter 3 Living to Eat or Eating to Live?   14

     Chapter 4 In the Community   21

     Chapter 5 Home   28

     Chapter 6 Cultures of the World   36

     Chapter 7 Health   42

     Chapter 8 Entertainment and the Media   49

     Chapter 9 Social Life   55

     Chapter 10 Customs, Celebrations, and Holidays   61

     Chapter 11 Science and Technology   68

     Chapter 12 The Global Consumer   76

Reading Placement Test   83

Quizzes for Chapters 1-12   94

Answer Keys for Tests and Quizzes   118

Introduction

Interactions 1 Reading encourages students to become actively involved in their own reading development. Students' thoughts and input are crucial in the reading process. They need to form ideas before reading a selection, pick out important ideas as they read, and finally, consider and discuss critically the main idea—the writer's message. The students are interacting with the reading selections, with the writers' ideas, and with others in the class.

The goal of **Interactions 1 Reading** is for students to become independent readers through instruction in the various reading skills and through intensive and extensive readings. There are pre- and post-reading exercises to develop reading skills and vocabulary. The exercises carefully introduce and model the key skills. Expansion and extension ideas provide additional challenging work to meet the individual needs of more advanced learners.

The reading level is challenging. The selections represent the different learning fields in order to prepare students to use academic textbooks. Students practice identifying main ideas, classifying and organizing information, and preparing summaries— skills needed for academic study and research. Although technical vocabulary may be pre-taught, students are encouraged to use context clues to infer meanings of new vocabulary. Sentence structures include complex and compound sentences that are common in academic texts. Finally, the reading passages express various cultural viewpoints and issues for analysis and class discussion.

General Teaching Suggestions

Teacher's Role

The reading teacher has a multi-faceted role. At times, the teacher needs to give instruction especially about language issues and provide cultural and background information that is important to the topic. Other times, the teacher is a participant listening to and sharing opinions and taking part in class and group discussions. The teacher is also a facilitator, creating a classroom environment that promotes learning and communication. Finally, the teacher provides encouragement and feedback, challenging students to continue developing their reading skills.

Teaching Practices

As your role as teacher changes in the classroom, you will want to adjust the practices you use. With whole-class activities, such as large group discussions and sharing of ideas, initial presentations, and comprehension activities, you need to keep students' attention.

- Use volunteers as models and then call on others in the class.
- List important information and words on the board.
- Maintain a lively pace in the class.
- Try to give everyone a chance to participate.

When checking comprehension of reading selections, begin with *yes/no* questions and *or-* questions, allowing the beginning level students to answer. Then ask information questions (*wh-* questions: *who, what, when, where, why*). Later, ask questions to the more advanced students that require more critical and creative thinking. These would be questions that involve analyzing, making inferences, and making comparisons. For example: *What would you suggest ...? How do you ...? Why would someone ...?* As you go through the reading selections, you may want to stop after each paragraph to check understanding and to point out and discuss key vocabulary words.

As you review the responses to the student book exercises, ask volunteers to explain their answers and to justify their responses. If appropriate, have the class look back at the readings to verify information and details. In exercises where more than one answer is possible, invite several students to share their responses and ideas.

Groupwork

Small groups allow students more of a chance to participate in discussion activities. It is often easier to speak in a small group than in front of the whole class, so the small group situation is more secure for those who are less proficient in their speaking skills. In addition, it allows time for students to help each other with vocabulary. Students can think and practice saying something in a small group before addressing a larger audience. Groupwork promotes discussion and sharing of ideas and cultural understanding. Students can learn from each other. Groupwork also allows you to address individual needs of students.

When students are working in groups, be sure that:

- students understand the directions of the activity
- everyone in the group is involved or has a role
- students show respect for each other
- there is a time limit for the activity
- groups have a chance to share what they discussed or prepared

Divide the class into groups of 4 - 6 for discussions and group writing activities. Prepare for groupwork. Have the following roles clearly defined for each member of the group:

- *reader*, or *facilitator*, who reads instructions, guides the group, is the leader
- *recorder*, who takes notes on discussions and answers for the activity
- *checker*, who makes sure everyone in the group understands points and watches the time, etc.
- *reporter*, who will share the group's information with the rest of the class

As groups are working, go around the room listening. You may need to assist with vocabulary or give other guidance. Your job is to facilitate the group activity, not to lead it. Make a note of types of problems that arise and address them later.

Vocabulary

Before each of the reading selections, students discuss what they already know about a topic area. Basic vocabulary is reviewed or presented in illustrations and in pre-reading questions. Make a list of words for students to refer to as they work through the chapter. Key vocabulary is listed before each of the readings. It is not necessary for students to study all of these words before doing the reading exercises, but it is helpful for them to check off the words they know and circle words that are new to them. You may want to have volunteers suggest meanings of words they know. Remind students to look for these key vocabulary words in the reading selections. Often there are context clues, restatements or definitions of the words within the selection. Encourage students to make general guesses about the meanings of the new words based on the context clues. Later, they may want to check a dictionary for the precise meanings. After completing the reading activities, have students look back at the vocabulary lists and check again their understanding of the new words. It is a good way for students to check their understanding and to check their own progress.

Multi-level Classes

Students have different needs and learning styles, so there will usually be a range of levels within a class. By varying the types of activities, you can address the needs of all students. Use whole class activities for presenting and modeling activities. Allow students to work individually, in pairs, or small groups to practice and prepare responses. During this time, give individual attention as needed. Have students work together in cooperative groups, not competitive groups. In this way, all students will participate, contribute, help, and learn from each other rather than competing against each other. If some students finish classwork activities before others in the class, encourage them to work on the expansion and extension suggestions found at the end of many of the student book exercises. You may want to provide additional reading materials for these advanced learners to browse through if they finish earlier than others. If possible, allow students to explore the Internet for related readings and information to share with the class related to the chapter topics.

You may want to ask students to evaluate their own progress halfway through the course. Ask them to write down if they feel they are making progress and what they feel they have learned so far in the course. Also ask them to write down what they hope to achieve in the second half of the course and how you can best help them achieve their goals. As you read through their self-evaluations, make notes about common goals they have to incorporate into the course. Give students feedback on their progress, too.

Using the Video

The video component provides additional activities related to the chapter topics. Each segment presents some culturally significant concept, fact, or issue. You may choose to use the video at the end of the chapter, as a culminating activity that reinforces listening, speaking, reading, and writing skills. The video section may be used at the beginning of a chapter to present the basic content area and initiate discussion of the basic content. Alternatively, you might find it more appropriate to use the video section to break up the heavy reading content and reading skills exercises in the chapter.

For each video segment there are several activities. The first exercise prepares students for watching the video. Students list vocabulary or share information that they know about the topic. They can make predictions about what they will see based on the title and the activity questions. The next two activities guide students as they watch the video at least two times. Students should read the questions before watching so they will know what information they need to find. The video segments are relatively short, so students are encouraged to watch the videos several times. The final video exercise invites students to check for other information related to the video segment in newspapers, magazines, and on the Internet. It leads students to read for information and to apply their reading skills to things outside of the classroom.

Administering the Reading Placement Test

The Reading Placement Test helps teachers and administrators place students into the Reading strand of the **Interactions Mosaic** series. All of the placement tests have been carefully designed to assess a student's language proficiency as it correlates to the different levels of the **Interactions Mosaic** series.

The Reading test has been created to assess both vocabulary development skills and reading comprehension skills. The first three parts of the test assess the skills students use to determine word meaning. Part 1 focuses on determining meaning and usage from context. Part 2 narrows in on idiomatic expressions. Part 3 determines whether students can scan for members of word families. The final part of the test, Part 4, assesses reading comprehension and consists of four different reading selections. The selections vary in length and complexity. Students must answer both literal and inferential questions.

The tests follow multiple choice and true/false formats for easy administration and scoring. Use the following charts to place your students in the correct level of text. To maintain test validity, be sure to collect all copies of the test and store the test in a secure location.

Placement Chart for the Reading Test

Number of Items Correct	Place in
0 - 10	Needs a more basic text.
11 - 17	Interactions Access
18 - 24	Interactions 1
25 - 34	Interactions 2
36 - 43	Mosaic 1
43 - 48	Mosaic 2

Using the Chapter Quizzes

The **Interactions 1 Reading** chapter quizzes allow teachers to assess whether the students have mastered the vocabulary and basic comprehension of the reading passages in the chapters. They also assess how well students can use the real-life reading skills or recognize word categories. In addition, they help assess how well students can use the language to communicate in writing their own ideas and thoughts about the chapter topics.

The **Interactions 1 Reading** chapter quizzes do not test students' reading comprehension or summarizing skills. The teacher should be assessing and evaluating students' reading skills progress as they do the exercises in the chapters.

The chapter quizzes also bring closure to chapters and give students a feeling of achievement and progress as they go through the textbook and course.

Description

There are twelve quizzes, one for each chapter in the reading text. Each quiz contains five sections:

- vocabulary
- comprehension
- grammar/structure
- real-life reading skills and categorization
- self-expression

The first section checks students' understanding of key vocabulary about the chapter topics. The vocabulary items are selected from the first two reading selections of the chapter. Students match the words with their meanings or synonyms.

The comprehension section checks general understanding of the key ideas of the first two reading selections of the chapter. The ideas are about the main ideas rather than specific details from the readings. Students decide if statements are true or false.

A major grammar or language structure for each chapter is highlighted in the third section of the quizzes. Students choose the correct form to complete sentences. Some structures tested include: simple present tense forms, prepositions, simple present vs. present progressive verb forms, pronouns, and related words (nouns, verbs, and adjectives). Although there are no exercises in the student book on these specific grammar points, students need to use them throughout the chapter exercises.

The fourth section of the quizzes focuses on the real-life reading activities of the chapters or other reading skills practiced in the chapters, such as categorization, facts and opinions, and sequencing. Students need to be able to recognize and use the words and expressions that are in reading materials around them daily and they need to apply other higher level reading skills.

The last section allows students to write their own personal views and responses to questions related to the chapter topics. The questions give students a

chance to reflect on their own experiences and feelings about the chapter topic. Answers will vary from student to student.

Administration

The quizzes can be duplicated and given to students individually or for full-class administration.

Scoring and Grading

Each section of the quiz is worth a specific number of points. The total possible score is 25 points.

School Life Around the World

Goals

- **Read about and discuss international students**
- **Understand main idea**
- **Recognize structure: paragraphs**
- **Identify topic sentences**
- **Read about and discuss college life around the world**
- **Use context clues**
- **Identify synonyms**
- **Summarize**
- **Understand school brochures and maps**
- **Express personal experiences and opinions**

Part 1 International Students

Before You Read

1 Discussing Pictures. Page 2.

Point out the three pictures and ask students to identify the people, places, and objects. Have students tell what the people are doing in each of the pictures. Then read the questions aloud and call on volunteers to answer. Encourage students to talk about things that are the same and things that are different from the pictures and their own school. Make a list of vocabulary on the board as students describe the pictures.

Sample Answers:

1. People: students, teachers, professors, instructors. Places: snack bar (snack room), classroom, hallway, registration/administration line. Other things: snack machines, tables, chairs, soda machine, books, signs; map, student desks, chalkboard, eraser, course listings, bookbag, program of studies, a line.

2. The first place may be in a dormitory or student lounge. It's a place for students to relax and talk. The people look like they might be from different countries. They are drinking coffee and studying.

   The second picture is in a school building, in classrooms. The students are studying or learning. They are listening and looking. The professors are teaching and explaining.

   The third picture is a registration line. The students are waiting in line to sign up (or register) for classes. They are looking at books and papers and talking.

3. In my school, there are soda machines and places to buy snacks. We have classrooms. We wait in line to sign up for classes. My school has different desks in the classrooms.

2 Thinking about the Answers. Page 3.

Read the questions aloud and call on volunteers to answer. Point out key vocabulary: *international students, institutions of higher learning, universities.* As students suggest answers, record students' responses and ideas on an overhead project or on a large piece of paper. You may want to review these responses later after students have read the selection.

Sample Answers:

1. International students are students who study in a foreign country. Colleges, community colleges, and universities are institutions of higher learning.

2. Most international students go to school in universities.

3. Some students attend colleges or universities far from home because they want to practice a new language, they want to study a particular subject, they have a scholarship, or the schools in their country may not offer advanced studies.

4. Colleges and universities want students from other countries because the students bring new ideas and enrich the school.

3 Vocabulary Preview. Page 3.

Read the words aloud and have student circle the ones they don't know. Students can look for the words they don't know in the reading. Have students check their understanding of the circled words after they complete the reading selection.

Read

4 International Students. Page 4. [on tape/CD]

Play the tape or CD as students follow along in their books. You may want to stop the tape or CD after every paragraph to check understanding and point out vocabulary words. Listen a second time as students read along.

Culture Note

Since there are so many different types of institutions of higher education in the United States, this level of education is available to nearly every post-secondary student. But, higher education is not free. All students pay tuition and other fees, although some do receive scholarships to help cover the costs.

After You Read

5 Recognizing Reading Structure: Readings, Chapters, and Paragraphs. Page 5.

Read the instructions. Refer to the book to show examples of chapters in books and paragraphs in reading selections. Have students look back at the reading on page 4 and indicate the number of paragraphs in this selection. Point out the letters for the various paragraphs. Students can complete the exercise. Go over the answers together.

Answers: 1. C 2. B 3. A 4. D 5. E

6 Understanding the Main Idea. Page 5.

Explain "main idea." Read the instructions and have students complete the exercise. Then discuss the answers with the whole class.

Answers: 1. T 2. F 3. F 4. T 5. F

Ask students to point out the information that is not true in the false statements. Students can look back in the reading selection for the correct information. Ask volunteers to restate the false statements to make them true.

Sample Answers:
3. High school and college graduates go to school in foreign countries for many reasons.
5. Some students may not like to go to school abroad. Colleges and universities want learners from other countries.

7 Finding Definitions in Context. Page 6.

Read together the instructions. Have students work individually in pairs to write the definitions of the words in Exercise 7. If some students finish before the rest of the class, ask them to find the definitions of the other vocabulary items. Go over the answers with the group.

Answers:
1. the other words in the sentence or paragraph
2. the meanings of new words and phrases
3. an institution of higher learning with one or more undergraduate colleges and graduate schools

4. a college student with a bachelor's degree or higher

5. a post-secondary student from another country

6. university, college, or school

7. in a foreign place

8. nations that don't yet have a high level or industrialization or technology

9. legal members of a nation or country

Students can develop definitions based on context clues in the reading for additional words (on pages 4 and 5).

Sample Answers:

College: an institution of higher learning

School: an institution of (higher) learning

Undergraduate: a post-secondary student without a college degree

Foreign: of a different country or culture

Tuition: the fee charged for instruction

Structure: organization or form

Chapter: the largest division of a book

Paragraph: a division or part about one idea or one kind of information

8 Answering Paragraph Questions with Details. Page 6.

Be sure students understand the difference between main idea and details. Read together the instructions. Ask students to complete the exercise. Go over the answers together.

Answers: 1. c 2. b 3. c 4. a

Discussing the Reading

9 Small Group Discussion. Page 7.

This activity allows students to use the vocabulary from the reading to talk about their own experiences related to the content. Arrange students in groups of four. Assign each person in the group a role:

Student 1: reading the questions to the group

Student 2: restating answers

Student 3: recording information

Student 4: reporting the answers to the whole class.

Model the activity and the four roles. Give the groups about 15-20 minutes to discuss the questions. Circulate among the groups, listening, and giving assistance as need. When all groups are finished, ask the reporters from each group to share the most interesting information form their groups.

Answers will vary.

Part 2 College Life Around the World

Before You Read

1 Vocabulary Preview. Page 8.

Read the words aloud and have students circle the ones they don't know. Encourage students to explain the meanings of the words they do know. Students may want to come back to this vocabulary section after reading the selection to check again their understanding of the circled words. Students can look for the word(s) in the reading selection and use context clues or look up the meanings of the words in a dictionary.

Read

2 Recognizing Topic Sentences. Page 9. [on tape/CD]

Read together the instructions and go over carefully the example. Then play the tape or CD as students follow along in their books. Stop the tape or CD after every paragraph and ask volunteers to read the sentence they underlined as the topic sentences. You may also want to check understanding and point out vocabulary words in each of the paragraphs.

Chapter 1

Answers:

A. In some ways, life on the campuses of institutions of higher learning is the same everywhere in the world.

B. Maybe student life is similar, but the system of higher education differs in countries around the world.

C. Teaching and learning methods and styles differ in various cultures, at different colleges and universities, and in individual courses.

D. At many institutions of higher learning, resources for learning and recreation are available to students.

and follow a plan or textbook. Some give a lot of homework and use quizzes and tests.

D. Many university and colleges have learning resources and recreational resources for their students. Some have libraries and learning resource centers for studying. Some have computers and audio and visual equipment for students to use. There are stores. Students can talk to advisors. Students can relax in snack bars, swimming pools, or sport resources.

After You Read

3 Learning to Summarize. Page 10.

Explain what a summary is. Read the instructions and call attention to the summary of Paragraph A. Compare and contrast the summary with Paragraph A. Arrange students in groups of four to practice summarizing. You may want to assign paragraphs to the groups. Allow 10-15 minutes for groups to read and summarize their paragraphs. Remind students that the topic sentence gives the main idea of a paragraph and the other sentences give details. Have a volunteer from each group read aloud its summary. If several groups have summarized the same paragraphs, compare and contrast the different versions. Discuss any differences.

Sample Answers:

B. There are many different systems of higher education used in countries around the world. In the United States, students can go to community colleges, state or private colleges, or universities. After that they can go to graduate school. In Iran, only students with the best test scores can go to universities. In Germany, most students go to universities or technical colleges.

C. There are differences in teaching and learning. Some teachers are very formal and others are casual. Some teachers have students work in groups. Others use lectures

Discussing the Reading

4 Small Group Discussion. Page 11.

Arrange students in groups of four to discuss their answers to the questions. Encourage students to refer back to the reading and vocabulary list for useful words and expressions. Give the groups about 15-20 minutes to discuss the questions. Circulate among the groups, listening and giving assistance as needed. When all groups are finished, invite students to share the most interesting information from their groups.

Talk It Over

This activity gives students a chance to express their own opinions and preferences about student life. Read together the instruction. Model expressing preferences. For example: *I prefer living with my family because I feel happy with my family. I don't like student housing. It's too noisy. I don't like apartment life. It's too much work...* Ask a volunteer to state his or her preference.

Arrange students in groups of four to talk about their own preferences. Allow 15-20 minutes for discussion. You may want to have groups report their findings. Were all their answers the same? For which topics were the answers similar? For which topics were the answers different? Students may write about their own preferences on student life using the answers they circled on the chart and adding details from their own lives.

Part 3 Vocabulary and Language Learning Skills

1 Finding Definitions of Vocabulary Items. Page 12.

Ask students to complete the exercise on their own. Then discuss the answers with the whole class. Encourage students to give their reasons for their answers. In pairs, have students practice the vocabulary. One student reads the definition of a word and the partner responds with the vocabulary word. Then have one student say a vocabulary word and the other student give a definition.

Answers: 1. i 2. d 3. b 4. a 5. e 6. j 7. f 8. c 9. g 10. h

2 Recognizing Words with the Same or Similar Meanings. Page 13.

Read the instructions and go over the example. Ask a volunteer to explain how the three words are similar and why the remaining word is different. Have students work individually on the exercise. Go over the answers and have students justify their answers.

Answers: 1. software 2. atmosphere 3. undergraduates 4. higher 5. individual 6. a cafeteria 7. the textbook 8. titles 9. technical 10. exit

3 Real-Life Reading: School Materials. Page 13.

In each chapter, there is a section about real-life reading materials related to the chapter topic. This section encourages students to notice and use reading materials that are readily available around them. Point out that the sample materials in the textbook may be slightly different from the materials they may see in their local environment.

Read together the instructions. Explain that using context clues to guess meanings of new words can save time. Review orally or write on the board some expressions or questions that can be used to ask the meaning of words, such as: *What does _____ mean? What's the meaning of _____? What the definition of _____?*

Begin reading the list of facilities and services. Stop and model asking about the meaning of some selected words. Encourage volunteers to suggest meanings or give examples to define the words.

Then ask students to look over the listing. They can underline words they know and circle words that they don't know. Have volunteers ask about words they circled. Invite others to suggest definitions or to explain the meanings. Students can talk about any experiences they have had or friends have had with the different places and services.

Have students practice asking and answering questions about locations of the facilities and services using the map. *Where can I buy a book? Where can I register for classes? Where can I get some coffee?*

4 More Real-Life Reading. Page 15.

You may want to have students do this exercise as a scavenger hunt by sending out students in small groups. Give them 15-20 minutes to see how many of the different types of reading materials they can find and bring back to class. Alternatively, you may want to have students do this as a homework assignment. Allow time for students to share the samples that they found and talk about vocabulary that they learned from the reading materials.

Part 4 Personal Stories and Humor

This part of the chapter provides lighter reading. Students can read the selections individually, in pairs, or small groups. Point out the titles of the readings and the illustrations. Have students make predications about the content based on the titles and illustrations.

1 Experiences and Opinions of College Life. Page 15.

Have students read the first selection. As a group, summarize the reading. Then ask questions about important details. *Where is the student from? What places does he enjoy on the campus? What does he like about the school? What doesn't he like? What is different about the school in the United States and schools in Germany? Do you agree with him? Why or why not?*

Repeat the procedure with the other two paragraphs. Ask questions about the content or have students prepare their own questions about the readings for others in the class to answer.

Have students write their own opinions of schools in the United States. Use questions to guide them as needed. *What do you like/don't like about schools in the United States? What is different about schools here and in your country? What are some problems that international students have in the United States?* Encourage students to share their writing with others in the class.

2 The Humor of Higher Education. Page 16.

Humor is culture-bound. Although students may understand the situations in the cartoons, they may not agree that they are funny. Explain that the cartoons are about commonly-accepted notions or beliefs about education and schools in the United States.

Read the first cartoon. Have students give their interpretations of the main joke. Guide them as needed. *Do students usually ask parents for assistance in understanding their lessons? What do you think about Norm's feelings about his father? Does this cartoon make you laugh or not? Why?*

Discuss the other two cartoons with the whole class or have students work in small groups to talk about their ideas. As a class, summarize the jokes and students' reactions to them.

Students can create their own cartoons about school humor or relate their own humorous story related to school.

Sample Answers:

1. First cartoon: Norm doesn't think his father can help him study for the test. Norm thinks that his father doesn't understand the college course or that his father is not intelligent.

   Second cartoon: Norm did not get a good grade in economics but thinks he is good enough to help someone else.

   Third cartoon: Norm was cheating on a test, but wrote the wrong answer. He feels sorry that he cheated, until he learns that his cheating didn't help him.

Culture Note
First cartoon: Students may think that Norm shows a lack of respect for his parents, so this might not seem humorous.
Second cartoon: Norm appears to be very arrogant. He assumes that he is qualified to help another person when he obviously does not know much about economics himself.
Third cartoon: Consequences and views of cheating may vary.

Video Activities: Exchange Students

Before You Watch
Read the questions aloud and ask students to discuss their answers in small groups. Have students report to the class their answers.

Watch [on video]
Ask them to read five questions. Then play the video and have them write their answers. Review the answers together.

Answers: 1. Turkey 2. 17 3. San Diego 4. a prom 5. sad to leave their U.S. families

Watch Again [on video]
Have students read the five statements. Replay the video and have students decide if the statements are true or false. Review the answers. Have volunteers correct statements that are false.

Answers: 1. F 2. T 3. T 4. F 5. F

After You Watch
Read together the explanation of phrasal verbs. Write some examples of phrasal verbs on the board such as sign up, look up, work out. Say a sentence using the verbs and have students suggest the meanings. *I need to **sign up** for classes.* (register) *I'm going to the library to **look up** information for a history paper.* (research) *Do you want to go to the gym to **work out**?* (exercise)

Have students read the sentences and match the phrasal verbs with their meanings. Go over the answers together.

Answers: 1. c 2. b 3. d 4. e 5. a

Experiencing Nature

Goals

- **Read about and discuss how weather affects people**
- **Understand main idea**
- **Read about and discuss global climate changes**
- **Summarize**
- **Identify synonyms**
- **Understand nature maps**
- **Express personal experiences and opinions**

Part 1 The Powerful Influence of Weather

Before You Read

1   Discussing Pictures. Page 20.

Arrange students in small groups to talk about the pictures. Have a volunteer from each group report their responses to the questions. Make a list of vocabulary on the board as students describe the pictures and talk about their weather preferences.

Sample Answers:

1. The first woman is tall, blonde, happy, old (middle-aged). She's wearing a hat, shorts, sandals, a sleeveless shirt/blouse, and glasses. She's carrying a ball. She's smiling because she's feeling happy and it's a sunny day. The young woman is sad. She's thin, athletic, short, brunette, dark-haired. She's wearing a tennis skirt and top, sneakers, and socks. She has a tennis racket and tennis ball. She's sad because it is raining (and she can't play

tennis). The boy is tall and thin. He has short hair. He's wearing shorts and a short-sleeved shirt. He has a rake. He's angry (annoyed, upset) because it's windy. He can't rake the leaves in the wind. The last person is short and has dark hair. He's wearing a snowsuit (jacket, snowpants), a hat, mittens, and boots. He's making a snowman. He's happy because he likes the snow.

2. In the first picture, it is sunny and hot. It's a nice day. In the second picture, it's raining. The weather is bad. It's cloudy. In the third picture, it is windy and cool. In the last picture, it is snowing. It is cold. I like warm weather because you can play sports outside.

Culture Note

You may want to use a map of the world and the United States during the discussion of weather conditions. Point out climate regions within the U.S. and have students tell about weather in their native countries and talk about typical temperatures for the various seasons.

2   Thinking about the Answers. Page 20.

Read the questions aloud and call on volunteers to answer. Encourage students to make guesses based on the topic of the chapter (weather) and clues within the questions. Point out key vocabulary: *wind, weather, health, moods.* As students suggest answers, record students' responses and ideas on an overhead project or on a large piece of paper. You may want to review these responses later after students have read the selection.

Sample Answers:

1. Biometeorologists are people who study weather and how it affects living things.

2. Wind can blow dust and smoke and make it difficult to breathe.

3. If the weather is nice, then people feel good. If the weather is bad, people may feel bad or sad.

4. In winter it is cold, so people stay inside. But people need to get outside and get fresh air. Maybe the winter makes people sad or sick.

3 Vocabulary Preview. Page 21.

As you read the words aloud, ask students to circle the ones they don't know. You may want to have volunteers suggest the meanings of the new words. Encourage students to look for the words in the following reading. After completing the reading selection, have students check their understanding of the circled words.

Read

4 The Powerful Influence of Weather. Page 21. [on tape/CD]

Play the tape or CD as students follow along in their books. You may want to stop the tape or CD after every paragraph to ask comprehension questions and to point out key vocabulary words. Listen a second time as students read along.

After You Read

5 Recognizing Paragraph Topics. Page 22.

Read the instructions aloud. Point out the example. Then have students complete the rest of the exercise. Go over the answers together.

Answers: 1. b 2. d 3. c 4. e 5. a

6 Understanding the Main Idea. Page 22.

Review "main idea." Read the instructions and have students complete the exercise. Then discuss the answers with the whole class.

Answers: 1. F 2. T 3. T 4. F 5. F

Ask students to point out the information that is incorrect in the false statements. Students can look back in the reading selection for the correct information. Ask volunteers to restate the false statements to make them true.

Sample Answers:

4. The atmosphere and weather affect people moods. People in the northern regions eat and sleep longer, usually work badly, are tired, and feel depressed.

5. According to scientists, the cause of health problems and sad moods may be the weather and the atmospheric conditions.

7 Finding Definitions and Words with Similar Meanings. Page 23.

After reading the instructions together, have students work individually to write the vocabulary words to complete the sentences in exercise 7. Go over the answers with the group.

Answers: 1. biometeorologists 2. atmosphere 3. snow, rain, humidity, air pressure 4. weather 5. stroke 6. sudden stopping of the heart 7. flu 8. lungs 9. emotional conditions and feelings 10. season affective disorder, mood disorder.

Students can look back at the reading on pages 21-22 for definitions of other vocabulary words.

Sample Answers:

Air pressure: the force of air

Emotions: feelings

Irritable: not very nice to other people

8 Recognizing the Main Idea. Page 24.

Read together the instructions. Remind students that details support or give examples of the main idea. Have students complete the exercise. Go over the answers together.

Answers: 1. d 2. d 3. a 4. d

You may want to have students answer the questions in Exercise 2 page 20 by giving details or examples from the reading selection.

Sample Answers:

1. Biometeorologists are scientists. They study how the weather affects the health and emotions of people.

2. Strong winds from the mountains may cause people to have more strokes and heart attacks. The winds can also cause headaches and asthma (breathing problems).

3. Changes in temperature can cause colds and flu. Very cold weather may cause diseases of the blood and heart attacks. Some people have more heart attacks in hot, humid weather.

4. Winter mood disorder can make people feel tired and nervous.

Discussing the Reading

9 Small Group Discussion. Page 25.
This activity allows students to use the vocabulary from the reading to talk about their own experiences related to the content. Arrange students in groups of four. Set a time limit for the small group discussions. As groups talk about their answers together, circulate among the groups, listening, and giving assistance as need. When all groups are finished, ask a volunteer from each group to summarize their ideas.

Answers will vary.

Part 2 Global Climate Changes

Before You Read

1 Vocabulary Preview. Page 25.
As you read the words aloud, have students circle the ones they don't know. Tell students to look

for these words in the next reading selection. After reading the selection, students can return back to this list and check their understanding of the circled words. Encourage students to use context clues or look up the meanings of the words in a dictionary.

Read

2 Paragraph Titles. Page 26. [on tape/CD]
Read together the instructions and go over carefully the example. Then play the tape or CD as students follow along in their books. Stop the tape or CD after every paragraph and ask volunteers to read the title they chose and identify the topic sentence. You may also want to ask some comprehension questions and point out key vocabulary words in each of the paragraphs.

Answers:
Paragraph Titles:
1. Climate in Regions of the Globe
2. General Changes in the Nature of Weather
3. Global Warming and the "El Niño" Effect
4. The Powerful Effect of People on Nature

Topic Sentences:
1. In different areas of the globe, the climate generally stays the same from year to year.
2. According to some meteorologists (weather researchers), the earth's climate is changing slowly.
3. Global warming and El Niño are having major effects of the earth's atmosphere, the weather, and the changing world climate.
4. Probably, human beings are the main cause of the extreme effects of weather and climate changes.

After You Read

3 Summarizing Paragraphs. Page 27.

Review what a summary is. Read the instructions and call attention to the summary of the first paragraph. Arrange students in groups of four to practice summarizing and assign paragraphs to the groups. Allow 10-15 minutes for groups to read and summarize their paragraphs. Remind students that the topic sentence gives the main idea of a paragraph and the other sentences give details. Have a volunteer from each group read aloud its summary. If several groups have summarized the same paragraphs, compare and contrast the different versions. Discuss any differences.

Sample Answers:

2. Some people think the earth's climate is changing. The weather is becoming more extreme with longer times of very cold weather and longer times of very hot weather. There are more storms, and the storms are stronger and more powerful.

3. Global warming and El Niño have affected the weather and climate. Global warming has made the temperature increase around the world. El Niño causes more rain and storms in the Americas. It also causes drought in parts of Asia. Northern regions have more cold weather and snow storms.

4. People also cause changes in weather and climate. Cars and factories create carbon dioxide. Coal and oil are burned which makes carbon dioxide. Plants and trees can use carbon dioxide, but people are cutting down many trees. The carbon dioxide affects the atmosphere and the weather.

Discussing the Reading

4 Small Group Discussion. Page 27.

Arrange students in groups of four to discuss the questions. Set a time limit of 15-20 minutes. Circulate among the groups, giving assistance as needed. Have a volunteer from each group summarize the most interesting points discussed.

Answers will vary.

Talk It Over

This activity gives students a chance to give their own opinions and to explain their beliefs. Read together the instructions. Model expressing opinions. For example: *I believe that ... I think that... I'm certain that ... I don't believe that... I'm not sure that...*

Arrange students in groups of four to talk about their own opinions about nature and weather statements. Allow 15-20 minutes for discussion. You may want to have groups report their findings. Were all their answers the same? For which topics were the answers similar? For which topics were the answers different? Students may write about their own beliefs and opinions using the answers they circled on the chart and adding supporting details from their own experiences.

Part 3 Vocabulary and Language Learning Skills

1 Recognizing Words with the Same or Similar Meanings. Page 28.

Ask students to complete the exercise on their own. Then discuss the answers with the whole class. Encourage students to give their reasons for their answers.

Answers: 1. real life 2. countries and cultures 3. condition 4. global 5. physical health 6. increase 7. science 8. common 9. air pressure 10. human beings

2 Recognizing Word Meanings. Page 29.

Read the instructions and go over the example. Have students work individually on the exercise. Go over the answers and have students justify their answers.

Answers: 1. d 2. f 3. i 4. b 5. g 6. c
7. j 8. e 9. h 10. a

3 Real-Life Reading: Nature Map. Page 29.

Read together the instructions. Review orally or write on the board some questions that can be used to ask the meaning of words, such as: *What is a _____? Where is a _____ on the map? What's an example of a _____?*

Begin reading the list of global nature and weather items. Stop and model asking about the meanings of selected words. Encourage volunteers to suggest meanings or give examples using the map on page 31.

Then ask students to look over the listing. They can underline words they know and circle words that they don't know. Have volunteers ask about words they circled. Invite others to suggest examples or to explain the meanings. Students can talk about any experiences they have in the different places or with different weather conditions. Have students practice asking and answering questions about climate and weather using the map on page 31. *Where is there snow? What islands are in the Pacific Ocean? What continents are on the Equator? Where are there rain forests?*

4 More Real-Life Reading. Page 32.

Ask students to bring in examples of other weather and nature reading materials. Students may also want to look for and print out examples from the Internet. Encourage students to share the samples that they found and talk about any new vocabulary that they learned from the reading materials.

Part 4 Personal Stories and Humor

This part of the chapter provides lighter reading. Students can read the selections individually, in pairs, or small groups. Point out the titles of the readings and the illustrations. Have students make predications about the content based on the titles and illustrations.

1 Three Views of Nature. Page 32.

Have students read the first selection. As a group, summarize the reading. Then ask questions about important details. *Where does the person live? What is the weather usually like there? What bad weather do they have sometimes? What damage do the storms cause? What do people think about the bad storms? Do you agree or disagree?*

Repeat the procedure with the other two paragraphs. Ask questions about the content or have students prepare their own questions about the readings for others in the class to answer.

Have students write their own opinions of weather and climate in the local area. Use questions to guide them as needed. *What do you like/don't like about the climate? How do you feel in different weather conditions? Why?* Encourage students to share their writing with others in the class.

2 The Humor of Nature. Page 33.

Read the first cartoon. Have students give their interpretations of the main joke. Have students share experiences they have had with bad weather on vacations. Guide them as needed. *How do the boys feel on Saturday morning? What happens when the weather changes? What problems do they have? When does the sun come out again?*

Discuss the other two cartoons with the whole class or have students work in small groups to talk about their ideas. As a class, summarize the jokes or ironic situations and students' reactions to them.

Students can create their own cartoons about weather humor or relate their own humorous story related to nature and weather.

Sample Answers:
1. First cartoon: The weather is terrible for camping all Saturday. When the boys get ready to go home, the sun comes out and the weather is nice.

   Second cartoon: The people dream of taking a vacation to a warm island with beautiful weather. When they look out the window, they realize they can't go on vacation because there is too much snow. They can't get out of the house to go on their trip.

Third cartoon: During the day, the boy lives the beautiful, quiet woods. When it starts to get dark, he realizes he is alone and lost. The woods don't look so nice in the dark.

Culture Note

Camping: Many Americans enjoy camping and hiking for exercise and to enjoy nature. Snowbound: Students may not be familiar with winter and snow conditions. Some parts of the United States receive over 10 feet of snow per year. Transportation, schools, and businesses can be closed depending on the amount of snow.

Video Activities: Winter Storm

Before You Watch

Read the questions aloud and ask students to locate the cities and states on a map of the United States and discuss their answers in small groups. Have students report their answers to the class.

Watch [on video]

Ask them to read two questions. Then play the video and have them write their answers. Review the answers together.

Answers: 1. d 2. snow, storm, icy, freezing, wind

Watch Again [on video]

Have students read the places and weather conditions. Then replay the video and have students match the places and conditions. Go over the answers.

Answers: 1. d, e 2. c 3. a 4. f 5. b

After You Watch

Have students find weather reports for cities and regions around the world. Student can use any media: newspaper, Internet, TV news, magazines. Ask students to prepare a brief description of the weather in their chosen place. Students can share their weather reports.

Living to Eat or Eating to Live?

Goals

- **Read about and discuss global diets**
- **Understand main idea**
- **Recognize supporting details**
- **Use punctuation clues**
- **Read about and discuss food facts**
- **Summarize**
- **Identify facts and opinions**
- **Categorize words**
- **Understand menus and food labels**
- **Express personal experiences and opinions**

Part 1 The Changing Global Diet

Before You Read

1 Discussing Pictures. Page 38.

Arrange students in small groups. Ask them to look at the pictures on page 38 and answer the questions. After the groups have finished their discussions, have a volunteer from each group report their responses. List vocabulary on the board as students describe the pictures. Help summarize the responses. Encourage students to identify specific items in the illustrations and to talk about items they have eaten and/or like.

Sample Answers:
1. The first picture is a food stand in an Asian community. There are people eating with chopsticks, chopping/preparing food, and ordering food. The second

picture is a supermarket or convenience store with food products. There are some frozen foods, international foods, and convenience/packaged foods. In the third picture, a family is preparing food at home and eating. They are probably in the kitchen. The mother is offering food. Others are eating, cooking, and preparing vegetables.

2. The foods are similar because they are all ready to eat or need very little preparation. The foods are different because they are representative of different ethnic groups, different methods of serving the food.

Culture Note

Immigration has contributed to the variety of ethnic foods available in U.S. cities and in other cities around the world. The three illustrations may represent different settings within the same city/neighborhood in the United States or settings in different countries. Ethnic foods are becoming more popular in the United States and most supermarkets have special sections for ethnic foods.

2 Thinking about the Answers. Page 39.

Point out the title of the reading selection, "The Changing Global Diet," and the illustrations on page 38. Then read the questions aloud and call on volunteers to suggest any ideas they have. Remind students that these questions will help guide them as they read the selection and work on the exercises. Point out key vocabulary: *fast foods, diet, convenience foods, nutritious.* As students suggest answers, record students' responses and ideas on an overhead project or on a large piece of paper. Encourage students to develop their own pre-reading questions about the reading selection. You may want to review these questions and responses later after students have read the selection.

Sample Answers:

1. A diet is a plan for eating.

2. The same or similar types of fast foods can be found around the world.

3. People might like quick and convenient eating places because you can get food quickly, you don't need to prepare it, you don't need to clean up afterwards, you can get a variety of different types of food. People might not like these places because the food is not always good for you and it might be more expensive than preparing your own food.

4. Fast foods are becoming more nutritious because of better rules about foods and food preparation. People want more salads and fruits which are more nutritious.

5. Eating customs are changing because people are more concerned about health and nutrition.

3 Vocabulary Preview. Page 39.

As you read the words aloud, ask students to circle the ones they don't know. You may want to have volunteers suggest the meanings of the new words. Encourage students to look for the words in the following reading. After completing the reading selection, have students come back to this list and check their understanding of the circled words.

Read

4 The Changing Global Diet. [on tape/CD]

Play the tape or CD as students follow along in their books. You may want to stop the tape after every paragraph to ask comprehension questions and to point out key vocabulary words. Listen a second time as students read along.

After You Read

5 Recognizing Paragraph Topics. Page 41.

Read the instructions aloud. Point out the example. Then have students complete the rest of the exercise. Go over the answers together. Then have volunteers change the topic statements into questions. Write the questions on the board or overhead.

Answers: 1. e 2. c 3. d 4. b 5. a

1. e. In what ways is the global diet changing?

2. c. Why do people choose to stay away from fast food?

3. d. How are convenience foods becoming more nutritious?

4. b. How is fast food the same around the word?

5. a. What are some definitions of the word *diet*?

6 Understanding the Main Idea. Page 41.

Read the instructions. Review the questions that the class wrote in Exercise 5. Point out that the five main idea statements in this exercise answer the questions. Read the question about paragraph A (What are some definitions of the word *diet*?). Ask students if the statement is true or false. Then have students complete the exercise. Discuss the answers with the whole class.

Answers: 1. F 2. F 3. T 4. F 5. F

Ask students to point out the information that is incorrect in the false statements. Students can look back in the reading selection for the correct information. Ask volunteers to restate the false statements to make them true.

Sample Answers:

1. The word diet has three basic definitions- "usual food choices", "an eating plan", and "go on a diet."

2. Fast food has a lot of variety around the world. Some examples are hamburgers, tacos, pizza, schnitzel, falafel, eggrolls, and sushi. The style of the nourishment

4.

5.

Next Page

and the atmosphere of the eating places don't differ much.

4. Fast foods and convenience foods are becoming more healthful. Restaurant items are sometimes grilled and there are more vegetables. Packaged items now contain less fat, sugar, salt, and so on.

5. The global diet is changing mostly in good ways. Many people buy fresh, natural foods at markets. More families cook at home. Many meals contain the necessary food elements There is a larger variety of food choices and preparation methods.

7 Getting Meaning by Using Punctuation Clues. Page 42.

After reading the instructions together, have students look for examples of the punctuation and italics in the reading selection. Tell students to work individually to write the words or phrases to complete the sentences in Exercise 7. Go over the answers with the group.

Answers:
1. diet 2. diet 3. fast food 4. universal
5. fast-food chains 6. fiber, vitamins, minerals
7. convenience foods 8. junk food 9. nutrition bars 10. natural food

Students can look back at the reading on pages 39-49 for definitions of other vocabulary words.

Model asking questions about the vocabulary words and responding with a complete sentence answer. Point out the examples on the bottom of the page. Have students practice asking and answering questions about the meanings of the vocabulary words in Exercise 7.

8 Recognizing Supporting Details. Page 43.

Read together the instructions. Remind students that details support or are examples of the main idea. Have students complete the exercise. Go over the answers together.

Answers: 1. a 2. c 3. d 4. a 5. b

You may want to have students answer the questions in Exercise 2 page 20 by giving details or examples from the reading selection.

Discussing the Reading

9 Small Group Discussion. Page 44.

This activity allows students to use the vocabulary from the reading to talk about their own opinions and preferences about food. Arrange students in groups of four. Set a time limit for the small group discussions. As groups talk about their answers together, circulate among the groups, listening, and giving assistance as need. When all groups are finished, ask a volunteer from each group to summarize their ideas.

Answers will vary.

Part 2 Facts about Food

Before You Read

1 Vocabulary Preview. Page 44.

Read the words aloud. Students can underline words they already know and circle the ones they don't know. Tell students to look for these words in the next reading selection. Students can return back to this list and check their understanding of the circled words after completing the reading selection. Encourage students to use context clues to guess the meanings of the words or look up the meanings of the words in a dictionary.

Read

2 Choosing Paragraph Titles. Page 45.

Read together the instructions. Have students match the short titles with the longer versions. Go over the answers.

Answers:

Food for Thought—Brain Foods and Other Nutrients for the Mind and Memory

The Fat of the Land—The Effects of the Changing Global Diet in Different Cultures

Food Fights—Opposite or Contrasting Views on the Best Eating Habits

Getting the Bugs Out—Cooking and Eating Insect Foods for Good Nutrition

3 Facts About Food. Page 45. [on tape/CD]

Play the tape or CD of the reading selection as students follow along in their books. Stop the tape or CD after every paragraph and ask volunteers to read the title they chose and identify the topic sentence. You may also want to ask some comprehension questions and point out key vocabulary words in each of the paragraphs.

Answers:

Paragraph Titles:
1. Food Fights
2. Food for Thought
3. Getting the Bugs Out
4. The Fat of the Land

Topic Sentences:
1. Everywhere on earth there are "food specialists" with different or opposite views on the best kinds of nutrition for various purposes.
2. Various ingredients and dishes affect the mind in different ways, and some kinds of nourishment have better effects on the brain than others.
3. For several reasons, insects are an important kind of food in the global diet, and they will become a more common ingredient in the future.
4. The growing similarities in diet and eating habits around the world are influencing people of various cultures in different ways.

After You Read

4 Learning to Summarize. Page 47.

Read the instructions and call attention to the question and summary of the first paragraph. Arrange students in groups of four to practice creating their own paragraph questions and summaries. You may want to assign paragraphs to the groups. Allow 10-15 minutes for groups to read and summarize their paragraphs. Remind students that the paragraph question asks a general question. For their summary, they will need to include a general answer and then some supporting facts, details, or examples. Have a volunteer from each group read aloud its summary. If several groups have summarized the same paragraphs, compare and contrast the different versions. Discuss any differences.

Sample Answers:
2. What kinds of nourishment help the brain and memory? Certain vitamins and nutrients help memory and thinking ability. The B-vitamins in dark green vegetables help memory. Lecithin in soybeans and grains also helps memory. High protein foods are better for the brain than sugar and carbohydrates.

3. How are insects good food sources? In many parts of the world, insects are served as snacks and sauces. Ants, worms, grasshoppers, and other bugs are cooked and eaten. They contain protein, vitamins, and minerals.

4. How has the changing global diet affected people of different cultures? People in different cultures are eating in different ways. In Japan, people eat more Western foods than before, such as meats, dairy products, and desserts. This causes more heart disease and other health problems. In the Czech Republic, people eat more fruit and vegetables than before. People are losing weight and living healthier lives.

Discussing the Reading

5 Small Group Discussion. Page 47.

Arrange students in groups of four to discuss the questions. Set a time limit of 15-20 minute. Circulate among the groups, giving assistance as need. Have a volunteer from each group summarize the most interesting points discussed.

Answers will vary.

Talk It Over

Read aloud the instructions. Explain the difference between facts and opinions. Have students work individually as they read through the statements and decide if they are facts or opinions. You may want to have students review their answers in small groups before discussing students' responses with the whole class. Were all their answers the same? For which statements were the answers similar? For which statements were the answers different? Students may write about their own facts and opinions about food and nutrition to share with the class.

Part 3 Vocabulary and Language Learning Skills

1 Recognizing Meaning Categories. Page 48.

After reading the instructions, go over the examples in the chart. Then arrange students in small groups to complete the categorization activity. Go over the answers with the whole class. Have students suggest other words for each of the categories.

Answers:

People: college students, citizens, teaching assistants, meteorologists, graduates, classmates, immigrants, foreigners, teachers, professors, language learners, scientists, researchers, doctors, specialists.

Places: school, a college campus, restaurants, desert regions, a classroom, the whole world, food markets, a university, European countries, mountain areas, a tropical island, developing nations, tennis courts, snack bars, continents, swimming pools.

Possible Foods: beef and pork, chicken and duck, hamburgers, sandwiches, sushi and tempura, candy and cookies, salads, vegetables, fruit, grains and breads, dairy products, potato chips, ice cream, shellfish, rice and pasta.

Human Conditions: sickness or illness, academic freedom, anger, mood disorders, perfect health, heart disease, headaches, high blood pressure, asthma, diabetes, flu or pneumonia, sadness or depression, emotions, hunger.

2 Specific Categories. Page 50.

Read the instructions and have students work individually on the exercise. Go over the answers and have students justify their answers. Students can create their own categories and items to practice vocabulary.

Answers: 1. d 2. g 3. h 4. c 5. b 6. e 7. f 8. j 9. a 10. i

3 Real-Life Reading: Menus and Food Labels. Page 50.

Read together the instructions. Review the questions that can be used to ask information about the menus and labels. Then ask students to look over the menu and labels on page 51. They should underline words they know and circle words that they don't know. Have volunteers ask about several words they circled. Invite others to suggest examples or to explain the meanings. Then arrange students in small groups to practice asking their own questions about the items on page 51.

4 More Real-Life Reading. Page 52.

Ask students to bring in examples of other menus, recipes, and food/nutrition reading materials. Students may also want to look for examples on the Internet. Encourage students to share the samples that they found and talk about any new vocabulary that they learned from the reading materials.

Part 4 Personal Stories and Humor

1 Food Groups. Page 52.

Have students make predictions about the content based on the title and illustrations in the exercise. Then ask students to read the first selection. As a group, summarize the reading. Ask questions about important details. *What are some food groups? What is the name of the "food group" that the writer belongs to? Where do the members live? What do the members want to buy and cook? Do you think they often eat in fast food places? Why or why not? What is important for a happy family life? Do you agree or disagree?*

Repeat the procedure with the other two paragraphs. Ask questions about the content or have students prepare their own questions about the readings for others in the class to answer.

Have students write their own opinions of food, nutrition and eating. Use questions to guide them as needed. *Do you think it is better for people to eat out often or to cook more at home? Why? What is your favorite type of food? Where do you eat for special occasions? What do you like to eat for special occasions? Are there some types of foods that you don't eat? If so, why don't you eat them?* Encourage students to share their writing with others in the class.

2 The Humor of Food. Page 54.

Read the first cartoon. Have students give their interpretations of the main joke. Have students share experiences they have had with getting foods from bottles and other containers. Guide them as needed. *What is the boy doing? What is in the bottle? What do you think is under the pile of ketchup?*

Culture Note

Ketchup (catsup) is a popular condiment for many American fast foods: hamburgers, french fries, hot dogs, and so on. Sometimes it is very thick which makes it hard to flow from a bottle. Some companies are now using squeeze bottles with smaller openings to prevent this ketchup problem. Discuss the other three cartoons with the whole class or have students work in small groups to talk about their ideas. As a class, summarize the jokes and students' reactions to them.

The Frugal Gourmet is a popular TV cooking show. The host shows how to cook many different types of dishes, but he is frugal or careful in spending.

Students can share their own humorous food stories.

Sample Answers:

1. First cartoon: The ketchup was slow coming out of the bottle, so the boy smacked the bottle to make it come out faster. Unfortunately, it all came out at once, so he has a lot of ketchup but can't even seen the food underneath.

   Second cartoon: The woman needs to use her cell phone to check what to buy at the store.

   Third cartoon: The man wants to leave out some ingredients, but he is the "futile" gourmet—the food will not be good if he cooks this way.

   Fourth cartoon: The cashier at the food store can tell a lot about the customers from the types of food and products they buy. She embarrasses the man by telling him about himself.

2., 3., 4. Answers will vary.

Video Activities: Treat Yourself Well Campaign

Before You Watch

Arrange students in small groups. Read the questions aloud and ask students to discuss their opinions about various types of food. Have students report to the class their answers.

Watch [on video]

Ask them to read two questions. Then play the video and have them write their answers. Review the answers together.

Answers: 1. fast food, fattening food
2. salmon with black bean sauce, low-fat pizza with extra vegetables

Watch Again [on video]

Have students read the statements and choices. Then replay the video and have students circle the correct answers. Go over the answers.

Answers: 1. b 2. c 3. d

After You Watch

Have students bring in menus from the local area or from the Internet. Ask students to prepare a brief description of the food choices and the types of food offered on their menus. In small groups, students can compare and contrast the menus and prices.

In the Community

Goals

- **Read about and discuss giving directions**
- **Recognize paragraph and whole reading topics**
- **Understand main ideas**
- **Find illustrations of word meanings**
- **Recognize relation of detail to the point**
- **Skim for topics and main idea**
- **Read about and discuss laws of communities**
- **Summarize**
- **Identify logical and reasonable statements**
- **Recognize similar meanings and meaning categories**
- **Recognize nouns and verbs**
- **Understand community service information and signs**
- **Express personal experiences and opinions about communities**

Part 1 How Can I Get to the Post Office?

Before You Read

1 Discussing the Picture. Page 58.

Arrange students in small groups to answer the questions about the picture on page 58. After the groups have finished their discussions, ask a volunteer from each group to report the group's responses. As students describe the pictures, list vocabulary on the board. Guide students to summarize the responses. Encourage students to talk about their own experiences related to asking directions and being in a new city or place.

Sample Answers:

1. The two travelers are visiting a new place. They are looking at maps and a brochure about the city. They don't understand the map or brochure or they can't find the place(s) they want to visit. They look confused.

2. The other people are explaining the directions and pointing in different directions. It looks like the people don't agree with each other because they look angry.

3. This situation happens to me. I prefer to use a map for directions. People sometimes ask me for directions. I tell them "I don't know."

2 Thinking about the Answers. Page 58.

Point out the title of the reading selection "How Can I Get to the Post Office?". Then read the questions aloud and call on volunteers to suggest possible answers and to make predictions about the reading. Remind students that these questions will help guide them as they read the selection and work on the exercises. Call attention to key vocabulary: *directions, body language, community*. Record students' responses and ideas on an overhead projector or on a large piece of paper. Encourage students to develop their own pre-reading questions about the reading selection. You may want to review these questions and responses later after students have read the selection.

Sample Answers:

1. People can make a map. They can tell you the directions. They can take you there. They can show you a map. They can point out the way.

2. If a person doesn't know the answer, he or she might not answer. The person

might tell you to ask another person, or he or she might just walk away.

3. Body language can help you find directions because people can point out the direction with their hands.

3 Vocabulary Preview. Page 59.

As you read the words aloud, ask students to circle the ones they don't know. Ask volunteers to suggest the meanings of the new words. Tell students to look for the words as they complete the reading. Later, have students come back to this list and check their understanding of their circled words.

Read

4 How Can I Get to the Post Office? Page 59. [on tape/CD]

Play the tape or CD as students follow along in their books. Pause the tape or CD after every paragraph to ask comprehension questions and to point out key vocabulary words. Listen a second time as students read along again.

After You Read

5 Recognizing Paragraph Topics. Page 60.

Read the instructions aloud. Point out the examples. Then have students complete the rest of the exercise. Go over the answers together.

Answers:

C. Directions in the American Midwest

D. Directions in Los Angeles, California

E. Directions in Greece

F. Directions in Yucatan, Mexico

G. The Conclusion: Body Language and Gestures

b. The reading tells about people giving directions in different cities and countries.

6 Understanding the Main Idea. Page 61.

Read the instructions. Read the question about paragraph A (*What is the point of the*

introduction to the reading material?). Review question words and question formation as needed. Then ask students to complete the exercise. Discuss the answers with the whole class.

C. *How do people give* directions in the region of the American Midwest?

D. *How do people give* directions in the city of Los Angeles, California?

E. *How do people give* directions in the European country of Greece?

F. *How do people give* directions in some areas of Mexico like Yucatan?

G. *What is the point of* the conclusion to the reading material?

In what ways *do people give* directions in various cultures around the world?

7 Correcting Information. Page 61.

Read the instructions aloud before having students complete the exercise. Encourage students to look back at the reading selection as they correct the statements.

Sample Answers:

1. If you don't carry a map when you travel, you have to ask for directions.

2. In Japan, people most often use landmarks in their directions.

3. In the flatlands of the American Midwest, people will tell you directions with distances.

4. In Los Angeles, California, the most common way to give directions is with times (minutes).

5. Even if visitors to Greece don't understand the Greek language, the people will usually understand because the Greeks give directions with motions or gestures.

6. In some parts of Mexico, people are very polite, so they don't want to say "I don't know" in answer to questions about directions.

7. All over the world, body language is easier to understand than words in sentences.

   In various cultures around the world, people give directions to travelers and tourists in various ways and by pointing.

8 Finding Illustrations of Word Meanings. Page 61.

After reading aloud the directions and example, have students complete the exercise. Go over the answers together.

1. landmarks: the corner, the big hotel with the sushi bar, the fruit market, the bus stop, the fast-food fried chicken place, and so on.

2. directions: straight north, turn right, go another mile, in a northeast direction, and so on.

3. distances: 2 miles, another mile, about 5 minutes, kilometer, block, and the like.

4. body language: facial expressions, gestures, motions, movements, pointing, and so on.

9 Recognizing the Relationship of Detail to the Point. Page 62.

After reading the instructions together, have students look for examples of the colons, commas, and quotation marks in the reading selection. Tell students to work individually to complete the exercise. Go over the answers with the group.

Sample Answers:
1. The writer's rule is: "Never carry a map."
2. Some advantages are you practice a new language, you meet new people, and you learn new customs.
3. Tourists are often confused in Japan because there are no street names.
4. Some illustrations of Japanese directions are: "Turn left at the big hotel." "Go past the fruit market."
5. In the American Midwest, people might give directions like: go north for 2 miles, turn right and go another mile.

6. People in Los Angeles don't give directions in miles, kilometers, or blocks because they don't know directions or distance.

7. Greeks seldom give foreigners directions in words and sentences because most tourists don't understand Greek.

8. A person in New York City will say, "Sorry, I have no idea," if he or she doesn't know the location of a place.

9. A polite resident of Yucatan doesn't say "I don't know" because it is more polite to stay and talk to a person.

10. A person gives directions with body language such as: facial expressions, gestures, motions, and movements.

You may want to have students answer the questions in Exercise 2 page 58 by giving details or examples from the reading selection.

Discussing the Reading

10 Small Group Discussion. Page 64.

Encourage students to talk about their own experiences with directions and being lost. Arrange students in groups of four. Set a time limit for the small group discussions. As groups talk about their answers together, circulate among the groups, listening and giving assistance as needed. When all groups are finished, ask a volunteer from each group to summarize their ideas.

Answers will vary.

Part 2 The Laws of Communities

Before You Read

1 Vocabulary Preview. Page 64.

Read the words aloud. Students can underline words they already know and circle the ones they don't know. Tell students to look for these words in the next reading selection. Students can return back to this list and check their understanding of the circled words after completing the reading selection. Encourage students to use context clues to guess the meanings of the words or look up the meanings of the words in a dictionary.

Read

2 Skimming for Topics and Main Ideas. Page 64. [on tape/CD]

Read together the instructions. Explain the purpose of skimming in this exercise—to determine the topic of each paragraph. Students will re-read the selection later for details. Have students identify the topics of the paragraphs. Go over the answers.

Answers: D, B, C, A

Play the tape or CD of the reading selection as students follow along in their books. Stop the tape or CD after every paragraph and have students choose the best statement of the main idea. Go over the answers.

Answers: A. 3 B. 1 C. 2 D. 1

You may want to replay the tape or CD and have students follow along again in their books. Ask some comprehension questions and point out key vocabulary words in each of the paragraphs.

After You Read

3 Learning to Summarize. Page 67.

Read the instructions together. Encourage students to use the topic phrases and main-idea statements from Exercise 2 (pages 65-66) as a starting point for their paraphrasing and summarizing. Arrange students in groups of four to practice summarizing. You may want to assign paragraphs to the groups. Allow 10-15 minutes for groups to read and summarize their paragraphs. Then, ask a volunteer from each group to read aloud its summary. If several groups have summarized the same paragraphs, compare and contrast the different versions. Discuss any differences.

Sample Answers:

B. Rules about driving are not the same around the world. In some communities, people can drive when they are 14 years old and in other places at 18 years old. Seat belts and helmets may be needed. There are sometimes laws about crossing the street in the middle instead of at the corner.

C. There are laws about individual activities such as drinking and smoking. There are age limits in some places and laws about drinking and smoking in public places. In some countries, there are religious laws about these activities. People do not always obey these laws about individual activities.

D. Some old laws do not make sense today, so people do not follow them. In New Zealand, a man can have as many wives as he has sisters. In other places, a man cannot hold hands with his girlfriend or even wife on the bus or train. These laws seem strange to us today.

Discussing the Reading

4 Small Group Discussion. Page 67.

Allow 15-20 minutes for students to work in groups of four to discuss their answers to the questions. Circulate among the groups, giving assistance as needed. Ask a volunteer from each group to summarize the most interesting points discussed.

Answers will vary.

Talk It Over

Read aloud the instructions. Point out that answers may vary. Ask students to explain their reasons for their responses. Then discuss laws that students know that they consider to be usual and interesting.

Part 3 Vocabulary and Language Learning Skills

1 Recognizing Similar Meanings and Meaning Categories. Page 69.

After reading the instructions, go over the examples in the chart. Ask students to give the category for 1—ways to travel. Point out that the words in 3 can be used to define the others or can be substituted in the same sentence without changing the meaning of the sentence. For example: *Every country has its own rules / laws / regulations*. Have students work on the exercise in pairs or individually. Then, go over the answers with the whole class. Have students suggest categories where appropriate and sentences for the words with similar meanings. Students can create their own sets of words with similar meanings and meaning categories to share with the class.

Answers: 1. C 2. C 3. S 4. S 5. S 6. C 7. C 8. S 9. C

2 Recognizing Nouns and Verbs. Page 69.

To review, have students brainstorm nouns and verbs. List the words on the board. Point out that nouns are names of people, places, or things. Verbs are actions or something you can do. Read the instructions together. Make sure students understand that some words can be used as both nouns and verbs. Ask students to look up the

examples in a dictionary to find the parts of speech. Point out the common suffixes that are added to verbs to make nouns: *-ment, -ion, -ence, -ent, etc.* Tell students complete the exercise, using dictionaries as needed. Go over the answers together. You may want to have students look through the reading for other nouns with related verb forms.

Answers: 1. travel 2. prefer 3. direction 4. turn 5. resident 6. measure 7. motion, gesture 8. expression, movement 9. murder, robbery 10. smoke, drink

3 Real-Life Reading: Community Services and Signs. Page 71.

If possible, bring in a local telephone book and point out the community services pages. Have students suggest types of help or services that people need in the community. Read together the instructions. Tell students to underline words they know and circle words that they don't know on the community services and signs. Then arrange students in small groups to discuss the meanings of new words and describe the purpose of the real-life pieces. Ask volunteers to summarize their group discussions.

Model asking questions about the community services and signs. Have volunteers answer using the information on pages 71 and 72. Tell students to work with a partner asking and answering their own questions about the services and signs.

4 More Real-Life Reading. Page 72.

Encourage students to look for and bring in examples of other real-life reading materials related to community and public places. Students can share their samples with the class and talk about any new vocabulary that they learned.

Part 4 Personal Stories and Humor

1 Community Preferences. Page 73.

Have students to make predictions about the content based on the title and illustrations in the exercise. Have students read the first selection. As a group, summarize the reading. Then ask questions about important details. *What is special about California? What do they grow there? What do they produce? Do many people live there? How do you know? What are some important ethnic groups that live in California? What are some bad points about California? What do you think about California?*

Repeat the procedure with the other two paragraphs. Ask questions about the content or have students prepare their own questions about the readings for others in the class to answer.

Have students write their own opinions about a community, city, state, or country. Use questions to guide them as needed. *What is your favorite place? What is special about this place? What types of activities do people do there? What other things do tourists enjoy there? What are some things that people don't like about this place?* Encourage students to share their writing with others in the class.

2 The Humor of Community. Page 75.

If possible, bring in some postcards from the local area or other places. Ask students to describe their favorite postcards.

Read the instructions together. Then ask students to look at the first postcard and identify the place. Have students give their interpretations of the joke about the seasons.

Culture Note

The four pictures represent natural disasters that occur occasionally in California. Discuss the other three cartoons with the whole class or have students work in small groups to talk about their ideas. As a class, summarize the jokes and students' reactions to them.
Students can create and share their own humorous postcards.

Sample Answers:

1. First cartoon: California.

    Second cartoon: Any island in the South Pacific.

    Third cartoon: Somewhere in the Southwest of the United States because of the highway and plan to build a tourist site. It's in the Southwest because the name of the town is Spanish.

    Fourth cartoon: From outer space looking down on the United States.

2. First cartoon: California does not have the typical four seasons: winter, spring, summer, fall. Its seasons are all disasters.

    Second cartoon: The postcard makes it seem like all islands look exactly the same in the South Seas, so the postcards all look the same.

    Third cartoon: Buena Vista will not be an old town because it hasn't been built yet. The people are just creating a tourist site.

    Fourth cartoon: The aliens believe that the people in California and New York don't notice or mind if others are different. The people in California and New York are all a little different themselves.

3. Answers will vary.

Video Activities: A Homeless Shelter

Before You Watch

Arrange students in small groups. Read the questions aloud and ask students to talk about their thoughts about homeless people in their small groups. Have students report to the class their answers.

Answers will vary.

Watch [on video]

Ask them to read three questions. Remind them to think about the questions as they view the video. Allow students to discuss their answers to the questions in small groups. Then, review the answers together with the whole class.

Answers: 1. because there are no emergency shelters 2. like a big temporary white dome 3. trying to raise $50, 000 by organizing fund-raising events

Watch Again [on video]

Have students read the statements. Then replay the video and have students fill in the correct answers. Go over the answers.

Answers: 1. 1,200 2. 58 3. $20,000 4. 100 5. motels 6. volunteer

After You Watch

Write on the board the adjective endings: *-able, -less, -ous, -ed*. Have students suggest different adjectives that have these endings, such as: *suitable, movable; careless, helpless; mysterious, nutritious; prepared, proposed*. Then have students complete the exercises. Go over the answers with the group.

Answers:
1. 1. portable 2. removable 3. homeless 4. ambitious 5. interested.
2. 1. homeless 2. interested 3. portable, removable 4. ambitious

Home

Goals

- **Read about and discuss the changing family**
- **Recognize paragraphs in time order**
- **Understand main ideas**
- **Use punctuation and phrase clues**
- **Recognize time details (facts)**
- **Read about and discuss family time**
- **Summarize**
- **Make predictions**
- **Recognize similar and opposite**
- **Recognize nouns and adjectives**
- **Understand classified ads**
- **Express personal experiences and opinions**

Part 1 A Short History of the Changing Family

Before You Read

1 **Discussing Pictures. Page 78.**
Point out the four pictures and ask students to identify the people, places, and activities. Then read the questions aloud and call on volunteers to answer. Encourage students to talk about things that are the same and things that are different from the pictures and their own family life. List vocabulary on the board as students describe the pictures.

Sample Answers:
1. The first picture is at the front door of a home and the husband and wife and saying good-bye and kissing before leaving for work in the morning. The second picture is in a living room with a large extended family relaxing together in the evening. The third picture is a small nuclear family sitting around the TV in the evening. The last picture is a mother and son eating dinner in the kitchen.

2. Answers will vary.

3. Family life is changing because there are so many different types of families now. Families don't do the same activities or live the same way because of jobs and economic conditions and life styles. Family life might change in the future by children spending more time away from school. Families will also probably become smaller with people having fewer children.

2 **Thinking about the Answers. Page 79.**
Read the questions aloud and call on volunteers to answer. Point out key vocabulary: *family, extended family, nuclear family, marriage.* As students suggest answers, record their responses and ideas on an overhead project or on a large piece of paper. Review these responses after students have read the selection.

Sample Answers:
1. An extended family includes more relatives than a nuclear family.

2. Families today include two-parent families, single-parent families, combined families (when parents marry after divorce), no-children families, and so on.

3. Families changed in the 20th century because of World War II and social changes. Families became smaller.

4. The 1930s and 1940s were difficult years for most families because of the Great Depression and World War II.

5. After World War II, people married and created families again and there were more traditional families.

6. The most common family forms around the world today are extended families and nuclear families although single-parent families are becoming more common.

3 Vocabulary Preview. Page 79.

Read the words aloud and have students circle the ones they don't know. Students can look for the words they don't know in the reading. Have students check their understanding of the circle words after they complete the reading selection.

Read

4 A Short History of the Changing Family. Page 79. [on tape/CD]

Play the tape or CD as students follow along in their books. Stop the tape or CD after every paragraph to check understanding and point out vocabulary words. Listen a second time as students read along.

> **Culture Note**
> Family structure and values are a reflection of a cultural group. During discussions, encourage an objective exchange of ideas as opposed to critical statements of the different types of family groups.

After You Read

5 Recognizing Paragraphs in Time Order (History). Page 81.

Read the instructions. Have students look back at the reading on pages 79 and 80 to complete the exercise. Go over the answers together.

Answers: A. family B. different kinds of families C. present changes in the structure of the family D. in the 1930s and 1940s E. in the 1950s (the next decade) F. changes in family structure G. continue to change in the future

6 Topic of the Whole Reading. Page 81.

After reading the instructions, have students choose the best statement of topic. Have students give reasons for their choices.

Answer: d

7 Understanding the Main Idea. Page 81.

Read together the instructions. Have students work individually in pairs to complete the questions. Go over possible answers with the group.

Sample Answers:
A. What are the definitions
B. What are
C. Why have there been
D. What happened to
E. What happened to
F. between 1960 and the end of the twentieth century
G. What will families be like; will family structure change

8 Correcting Information. Page 82.

Be sure students understand the instructions. Students can look back at the reading as they complete the exercise. Go over the answers together.

Sample Answers:
1. The extended family is different from the nuclear family: it consists of many relatives (grandparents, parents, children, cousins, etc.) living in the same house.
2. There are many kinds of families on planet earth today including traditional nuclear family, single-parent family, foster family, etc.
3. In the early 1900s in the United States (and later in other countries), the divorce

rate began to rise and the birthrate began to decline; couples were staying married for fewer years and having fewer children.

4. Before and during World War II, families faced more financial problems in the industrialized world, so women had to work outside the home. Families were not "perfect."

5. After the war, family structure changed back in the other direction: there were fewer divorces and more stay-at-home mothers; children began living at home longer.

6. From the 1960s on, there were more new changes in the structure of the family around the globe.

7. Some people want the traditional two-parent nuclear family—with a working father and a mother at home; however, this structure will probably not come back and more family forms will appear on the earth.

In the twentieth century, there were many changes in the structure of the family; in the next century, there will probably be more changes, too.

9 Using Punctuation and Phrase Clues. Page 82.

As you read through the instructions, ask students to locate examples of the various types of punctuation and phrases in the reading selection on pages 79-80. Have volunteers identify the punctuation in the example. Then have students complete the exercise with their own definitions. If students finish early, have them create their own definitions of the additional vocabulary items. Go over the answers together.

Answers:

1. groups with a common ancestor
2. from the distant past
3. living in the same house or close together on the same street or in the same area

4. parents and their biological or adopted children
5. stays at home
6. one parent
7. divorced or widowed men and women who marry again and live with the children of their previous or earlier marriages
8. legal endings compared to the number of marriages
9. husbands were away at war
10. ten years

10 Recognizing Time Details (Facts). Page 83.

Read together the instructions. Students can look back at the reading for examples of the time expressions. Then have students match the events with the time expressions. Go over the answers. You may want to have students practice asking and answer *When* questions about the events. *When did many families have money problems, so more women began to work outside the home?*

Answers: 1. e 2. a 3. c 4. g 5. d 6. b 7. f 8. h

Discussing the Reading

11 Small Group Discussion. Page 84.

Arrange students in groups of four. Give the groups about 15-20 minutes to discuss the questions. Circulate among the groups, listening and giving assistance as needed. When all groups are finished, ask reporters from each group to share the most interesting information from their groups.

Answers will vary.

Part 2 Time with the Family—Past and Present

Before You Read

1 Vocabulary Preview. Page 85.

Read the words aloud and have students circle the ones they don't know. Encourage students to explain the meanings of the words they do know. After reading the selection, have students look back at the vocabulary words to check again their understanding. Students can use context clues from the reading or look up the meanings of the words in a dictionary.

Read

2 Knowing Time and Place in History. Page 85. [on tape/CD]

Read together the instructions and review the purpose of skimming in this exercise—to determine the topic of each paragraph. Students will re-read the selection later for details. Have students skim the paragraphs and identify the topics of the paragraphs. Go over the answers.

Answers: B, C, A, D

Play the tape or CD of the reading selection as students follow along in their books. Stop the tape or CD after every paragraph and have students choose the best statement of the main idea. Go over the answers.

Answers: A—1 B—3 C—2 D—2

You may want to replay the tape or CD and have students follow along again in their books. Ask some comprehension questions and point out key vocabulary words in each of the paragraphs.

After You Read

3 Learning to Summarize. Page 88.

Review what a summary is. Read the instructions and call attention to the paraphrases of the

important vocabulary. Then, compare and contrast the summary with Paragraph A. Students can work in groups of four to summarize assigned paragraphs. Remind groups that the topic sentence gives the main idea of a paragraph and the other sentences give details. Allow 10-15 minutes for groups to prepare their summaries. Have a volunteer from each group read aloud its summary. If several groups have summarized the same paragraphs, compare and contrast the versions. Discuss any differences.

Sample Answers:

B. The Japanese family in the 1900s was traditional. The wife usually stayed home with the children and the father supported the family financially. Parents usually arranged their children's marriages. Often extended families lived in the same house.

C. Neighborhoods were like extended families in some twentieth century communities. . There were different types of families in the neighborhood, but everyone knew each other and families were in close contact.

D. In today's world, changes in the typical family create some difficulties. There are many single-parent and divorce families. Families can get help from relatives and communities to help improve their lives.

Discussing the Reading

4 Small Group Discussion. Page 88.

Encourage students to refer back to the reading and vocabulary list for useful words and expressions as they discuss their answers to the questions. Allow 15-20 minutes to discuss the questions. Circulate among the groups, listening and giving assistance as needed. When all groups are finished, invite students to share the most interesting information from their groups.

Talk It Over

This activity gives students a chance make predictions about future family trends. Read together the instructions. Model expressions for talking about future possibilities. For example:

I think that families will become smaller. I don't believe that divorce will increase to 100%. I hope that ... If families become smaller, then there will be... It would be good if familes....

Arrange students in groups of four to talk about their own predictions. Allow 15-20 minutes for discussion. You may want to have groups report their findings. Were all their answers the same? For which items were the answers similar? For which topics were the answers different? Students may write about their own predictions on family life using the answers they marked on the chart and adding reasons for their predictions.

Part 3 Vocabulary and Language Learning Skills

1 Recognizing Similar and Opposite Meanings. Page 90.

Ask students to complete the exercise on their own. Then discuss the answers with the whole class. Encourage students to give their reasons for their answers. Students can find other pairs sets of words with similar or opposite meanings.

Answers: 1. S 2. O 3. S 4. O 5. S 6. O 7. O 8. O 9. S 10. O 11. O 12. S 13. S 14. S 15. O 16. O 17. S 18. S 19. O 20. O

2 Recognizing Nouns and Adjectives. Page 91.

Read the instructions and go over the examples of nouns and related adjectives. Provide other examples as needed (*married, marriage; universe, universal; custom, customary*). Review the function of nouns and adjectives in sentence structures. Go over the model. Then, have students work individually on the exercise. Go over the answers.

Answers: 1. community, family, social 2. human, related, ancestor 3. China,

property, equal 4. European, custom, powerful 5. younger, education 6. arranged, marriages, choice 7. history, nuclear, frequent 8. reason, decrease, economic 9. global, industrialization, universal 10. modern, institutions, protection

Tell students to complete the chart with nouns and related adjectives. Students can practice using the forms in sentences to talk about family customs and traditions around the world.

Answers:
Related Adjectives: common, familiar, social, human, ancestral, Chinese, proper, equal, European, customary
Nouns: power, youth, education, arrangement, marriage, choice, nucleus, frequency, reason, decrease

3 Real-Life Reading: Classified Ads. Page 92.

You may want to bring in some examples of classifieds from local papers and magazines. Remind students to use context clues to guess meanings of new words. Read together the instructions.

Have students look over the ads and match them to the categories. Go over the answers.

Students can reread the ads and underline words they know and circle words that they don't know on the ads. Have volunteers ask about words they circled. Invite others to suggest definitions or to explain the meanings. Students can summarize the purpose of each of the ads by answering the questions on page 93. Encourage students to talk about any experiences they have had or that friends have had reading or using classified ads.

Answers: A. 1 B. 2 C. 3 D. 3 E. 2 F. 4 G. 4 H. 5 I. 4 J. 5

4 More Real-Life Reading. Page 94.

You may want to have students do this exercise as a scavenger hunt by sending out students in small groups. Give them 15-20 minutes to see how many of the different types of reading materials they can find and bring back to class.

Students can also check school bulletin boards for ads. Alternatively, you may want to have students do this as a homework assignment. Allow time for students to share the samples that they found and talk about vocabulary that they learned from the reading materials.

Part 4 Personal Stories and Humor

1 Two Very Different Family Housing Situations. Page 94.

Have students read the first selection. As a group, summarize the reading. Then ask comprehension questions. *Where did the family live before they moved? Why weren't they happy in the apartment? Was it easy or difficult to find a house to buy? What were some problems with houses they looked at? What is a "fixer-upper?" What didn't the family like about the house? How did they make it better?*

Repeat the procedure with the other paragraph. Ask questions about the content or have students prepare their own questions about the readings for others in the class to answer. *What problems has this person had in life? How old is he now? Where does he live now? How does he survive? Why is he writing a book? Do you think he will succeed in getting a home? Why or why not?*

Have students write their own opinions of families and homes in the United States. Use questions to guide them as needed. *What do you like/don't like about where you live now? How important is your family to you? What changes would you like in your family or living place? What advantages or disadvantages do you see if American families and homes?* Encourage students to share their writing with others in the class.

2 The Humor of the Family. Page 96.

Have students look at the illustration as you read aloud the conversation between the husband and wife. Have students give their interpretations of

the main joke. Guide them as needed. *What work does the mother do during the day? Do you think the husband appreciates the work she does? Which "job" doesn't the wife want to do? What does she mean by that? Why do you think she says that?*

Discuss the other four conversations and pictures with the whole class or have students work in small groups to talk about their ideas. As a class, summarize the jokes and students' reactions to them.

Students can create their own conversations or relate their own humorous story about family life.

Sample Answers:
Conversation 1: A husband and wife are speaking. They are talking about the wife's many jobs. The wife's line has the joke. The joke is that the wife doesn't want to be a wife any more, possibly because the husband doesn't help with the care of the rest of the family.

Culture Note
Although divorce and separation are commonly accepted in some cultures, in others it is forbidden or disgraceful to the family and relatives. The role of the wife and mother varies from culture to culture.

Conversation 2: A babysitter is talking with the kids he/she is watching. They are talking about all the things they have done since the mother left. The babysitter can't think of anything else to do. The joke is that the mother has only been gone for ten minutes.

Culture Note
A babysitter is often a young teenager who is paid by the parents to take care of their kids while they are out. Usually the teenager is a neighbor or person from the local neighborhood.

Conversation 3: A mother and daughter are talking. The daughter has a boyfriend. Since the mother doesn't want to invite the boyfriend for dinner, the daughter plans to go over to his house and cook for him. The mother changes her mind and says he can come for dinner. The mother wants to know what her daughter is doing and she wants to make sure her daughter behaves appropriately.

Culture Note

Although some American parents would allow their children to visit a boyfriend/girlfriend unchaperoned, others prefer to monitor more closely their children's dating and social activities.

Conversation 4: A father and son are talking. The father is concerned about his son and asks what the problem is. The son mumbles something unclearly (You can't understand.), but the father can't understand the son's response. The joke is that the father finally says that he doesn't understand.

Culture Note

This conversation illustrates how parents often don't understand their children. The son is somewhat disrespectful in his sloppy speech and his loud response to his father. The father seems truly concerned about his son, but the son does not want to talk to his father.

Conversation 5: The conversation is between two friends. They are probably older people (50s or 60s). They are talking about the children with the one woman. Her friend assumes that they are her grandchildren, but they turn out to be her own children. The joke focuses on the fact that people are having children later is life rather than in their 20s.

Video Activities: Dust Mites

Before You Watch

Read the questions aloud and ask students to discuss their answers in small groups. Have students report to the class their answers.

Sample Answers:
1. Asthma is a lung disease. A person with asthma coughs and has difficulty breathing. It can be caused by allergies to dust, fur, feathers, etc. Other types of asthma can be caused by colds, lung infections, smoking, and food or drug allergies. You can treat asthma with inhalers (drugs that you breath into your lungs). Tests can be done to determine the exact cause of the asthma and then the person can avoid the problem substances.
2. A "dust mite" is an insect that is very small.
3. People can reduce dust by not wearing shoes in the house, cleaning and dusting regularly, and using wooden or linoleum floors.

Watch [on video]

Ask them to read the five questions. Then play the video and have them write their answers. Review the answers together.

Answers: 1. clean, bare, open 2. very small 3. c 4. uses plastic mattress covers, washes the bedding, doesn't have carpets, doesn't have curtains 5. hang the bedding out in the sun to dry

Watch Again [on video]

Have students read the three discussion questions. Then replay the video and have students talk about their answers in groups. Ask a volunteer in each group to report the group's responses.

Answers will vary.

After You Watch

You may want to assign this for homework. Go over the answers together. Arrange students in pairs to role play a person asking a doctor about dust mites. One student can ask the questions and the other student will play the role of the doctor answering the questions with the information from the research.

Sample Answers:

1. Dust mites are tiny bugs that live in houses. They cause allergies and asthma.

2. Dust mites live in warm, dusty, humid areas. So they live in pillows, mattresses, carpets, and furniture.

3. You can reduce the number of dust mites in bedrooms by putting plastic covers on mattresses and pillows. You should wash sheets and blankets every week.

4. You should have a hardwood, tile, or linoleum floor because they are easier to clean. If you have a carpet, don't put it on top of a concrete floor. You can clean a carpet with a special solution (3% tannic acid) every two months. (But it's better to get rid of the carpet.)

5. You can also vacuum carpets and furniture. Use plastic or wood furniture so less dust will collect on it. Keep the humidity low in the house.

Chapter 6

Cultures of the World

Goals

- **Read about and discuss the meanings of "culture"**
- **Understand conversation in paragraph form**
- **Understand main points**
- **Use context to figure out new vocabulary**
- **Recognize details of opinions**
- **Read about and discuss cross-cultural differences**
- **Summarize**
- **Give opinions**
- **Recognize nouns, verbs, and adjectives**
- **Use adverbs of manner**
- **Understand calendar notices and announcements**
- **Express personal experiences and opinions**

Part 1 Cross-Cultural Conversation

Before You Read

1 **Discussing the Picture. Page 100.**
Arrange students in small groups to discuss the picture. Have a volunteer from each group report their responses to the questions. List vocabulary on the board.

Sample Answers:
1. There are people from several different cultural/ethnic groups sitting around a table talking about important parts of their cultures. There are some business men (or

professors) and some students. Different types of architecture are pictured. The people are eating different ethnic foods.

2. There's an American, an Egyptian, a Hispanic, and an Indian. The first person on the left might be French (because there's a glass of wine). The second person might be German (because of the beer stein). The third might be Indian (because he's thinking of the Taj Mahal and wearing a Nehru jacket and has a calm, serene expression). The fourth is probably American (because of his causal clothes and casual position on the chair). The fifth might be American but could also be Japanese (because of the skyscrapers and the hamburger and fries and food in front of him). The fifth might be Mexican (because of the tacos and fiesta). The sixth could be Egyptian (because of the pyramids and espresso coffee).

3. The people are probably all talking about the good points of their cultures. Everyone's culture is different.

2 **Thinking about the Answers. Page 100.**
Read the questions aloud and point out key vocabulary: *cultural legacy, achievements, ancient cultures, universal.* Encourage students to make guesses based on the topic of the chapter (cultures) and clues within the questions. Record students' responses and ideas on an overhead project or on a large piece of paper. You may want to review these responses later after students have read the selection.

Sample Answers:
1. A "cultural legacy" from the past is the ideas, traditions, and customs that come from past or ancient cultures. It might include architecture, art, religion, philosophy, customs, traditions, food, dance, music, folk stories, medicine, etc.

2. Technical achievements from ancient cultures include transportation, aqueducts

(water systems), weapons, tools, writing methods, time keeping (clocks, calendars), etc. Scientific achievements include medicine, astronomy, etc.

3. Culture might be universal because ideas and inventions are exchanged around the world. There is more contact between different cultural groups than in the past. Most cultures want modern communication and industrialization.

4. Modern cultures vary around the world in language, gestures, social rules, and customs.

5. "Culture" can be viewed as being cultural history, ancient traditional culture, global culture, and cultural diversity.

3 Vocabulary Preview. Page 100.

As you read the words aloud, tell students to circle the ones they don't know. Ask volunteers to suggest the meanings of the new words. Encourage students to look for the words in the following reading. After completing the reading selection, have students check their understanding of the circled words.

Read

4 Cross-Cultural Conversation. Page 102. [on tape/CD]

Play the tape or CD as students follow along in their books. Stop the tape or CD occasionally to ask comprehension questions and to point out key vocabulary words. Listen a second time as students read along again.

After You Read

5 Recognizing Conversation in Paragraph Form. Page 103.

Read the instructions aloud. If needed, point out the words that the different speakers say in the conversation. Then have students complete the exercise. Go over the answers together.

Answers: 1. the long cultural legacy of the arts in European history 2. humanity's scientific and technological discoveries and achievements 3. the cultural sameness and similarities among modern peoples 4. cultural diversity—how groups vary in their styles and customs 5. different cultural ways of discussing ideas and telling opinions

Topic or subject of the whole reading: c

6 Understanding the Point. Page 104.

Read the instructions and have students complete the exercise. Then discuss the answers with the whole class.

Sample Answers: 2. included; achievements and discoveries 3. want; modern; everybody 4. more significant; appreciate and enjoy 5. cultures; different; a variety of

7 Figuring Out New Vocabulary from Context. Page 105.

After reading the instructions together, have students work individually using context clues to define the vocabulary words. Go over the answers with the group.

Answers:

1. Some examples of architecture are cathedrals and castles. Features of modern architecture include design and building styles. A

2. Civilization began in the Middle East and Africa over five thousand years ago. Ancient civilizations had astronomy, mathematics, medicine, and government. C

3. A legacy comes from the past. A legacy might include cities, governments, tools, and weapons. B

4. Modern things can be part of culture. People that like classical art and music will not agree with him. Kevin and Jade have very different opinions. A

5. Some examples of the worldwide media are movies, TV, CDs, the Internet, newspapers, and magazines. The media

gives people around the world the same information, music, and jokes. C

Students can look back at the reading on pages 102-103 for definitions of other vocabulary words.

8 Recognizing the Details of Opinions. Page 107.
Read together the instructions. Remind students that there are several answers for each question. Have students complete the exercise. Go over the answers together. Have students find specific references from the reading selection to support the answers.

Answers: 1. b, c, e, f 2. b, c, d, e 3. c, e, f 4. a, b, c, d, e, f 5. a, b, c, d, e, f

Discussing the Reading

9 Small Group Discussion. Page 108.
This activity allows students to use the vocabulary from the reading to talk about their own experiences related to the content. Arrange students in groups of four. Set a time limit for the small group discussions. As groups talk about their answers together, circulate among the groups, listening and giving assistance as needed. When all groups are finished, ask a volunteer from each group to summarize their ideas.

Answers will vary.

Part 2 Clues to World Cultures

Before You Read

1 Vocabulary Preview. Page 109.
As you read the words aloud, have students circle the ones they don't know. Tell students to look for these words in the next reading selection and use context clues to help guess their meanings. After reading the selection, students can return

back to this list and check their understanding of the circled words.

Read

2 Clues to World Cultures. Page 109. [on tape/CD]
Read together the instructions. Then play the tape or CD as students follow along in their books. Stop the tape or CD after each of the readings for students to select the topics. Then replay the tape, stopping at the end of each section for students to answer the questions. In addition, you may also want to point out key vocabulary words in each of the selections.

Answers:
Topics:
A: concepts of time and timing-doing things in a certain order or at the same time
B: visiting a family at home; eating and drinking with people from other cultures
C: body language-gestures, hand movements, and facial expressions

Point of the Material:
a: 1. b 2. b 3. a
b: 1 c 2. b 3. a
c: 1. a 2. c 3. c

After You Read

3 Learning to Summarize. Page 112.
Review what a summary is. Read the instructions aloud. Arrange students in groups of four to practice summarizing. Assign paragraphs to the groups. Allow 10-15 minutes for groups to read and summarize their paragraphs. Have a volunteer from each group read aloud its summary. If several groups have summarized the same paragraphs, compare and contrast the different versions. Discuss any differences.

Sample Answers:
A In some cultures, it is polite for people to wait their turn. Time and timing are important. In other cultures, it is important to

greet and ask for attention right away even if others are present. An Irish woman was patiently waiting her turn in a Latin American pharmacy and became annoyed when other customers entered and were served before her. In Irish culture it is important to wait one's turn, but in the Latin American culture it is important to greet people when entering a place.

B Customs for eating and drinking with people from other cultures, especially in a family's home, vary from culture to culture. In some places, the guest needs to tell the host when they are ready to eat. The host continues to serve food until the guest leaves food on the plate. In other places, these would be very impolite things for a guest to do.

C Body language varies from one culture to another. Hand gestures for may be fine in one country but may be considered to be rude or offensive in other countries.

Discussing the Reading

4 Small Group Discussion. Page 112.

Arrange students in groups of four to discuss the questions. Set a time limit of 15-20 minute. Circulate among the groups, giving assistance as needed. Have a volunteer from each group summarize the most interesting points discussed.

Answers will vary.

Talk It Over

This activity gives students a chance to talk about their own cultural attitudes and beliefs. Read together the instructions. Arrange students in groups of four to talk about their own cultures. Allow 15-20 minutes for discussion. You may want to have groups report their findings. Were all their answers the same? For which topics were the answers similar? For which topics were the answers different? Students may write about their own beliefs and opinions using the answers they

circled on the chart and adding supporting details from their own experiences.

Answers will vary.

Part 3 Vocabulary and Language Learning Skills

1 Recognizing Nouns, Verbs, and Adjectives. Page 114.

As you read the instructions aloud, call attention to the chart and clarify the function of nouns, verbs, and adjectives. If needed, have students identify nouns, verbs, and adjectives in other sentences before completing the exercise. Point out the related words in the boxes next to each item in the exercise. Ask students to complete the exercise on their own. Then discuss the answers with the whole class.

Answers:

2. describe (verb), description (noun), descriptive (adjective)
3. excellence (noun), excel (verb), excellent (adjective)
4. experienced (adjective), experience (verb), experiences (noun)
5. civilization (noun), civilize (verb), civilized (adjective)
6. invent (verb), inventive (adjective), inventions (noun)
7. agree (verb), agreeable (adjective), agreement (noun)
8. society (noun), social (adjective), socialize (verb)
9. contradict (verb), contradictory (adjective), contradiction (noun)
10. develop (verb), development (noun), developing (adjective)

2 Using Adverbs of Manner. Page 116.

Read the instructions and go over the example. Point out that for adjectives that end with the letter *y*, change the *y* to *i* before adding the *-ly*. For example: happy—happily. Adjectives that end in *-ic*, add *-al* before adding the *-ly*. For example: fantastic—fantastically. Have students work individually on the exercise. Go over the answers.

Answers: 1. proudly 2. loud 3. easily 4. amazingly 5. agreeably 6. scientific 7. human 8. polite 9. softly 10. forcefully

3 Real-Life Reading: Calendar Notices and Announcements. Page 118.

Read together the instructions. Then ask students to match the notices with the kinds of events. Students should underline words they know and circle words that they don't know. Have volunteers ask about words they circled. Invite others to suggest examples or to explain the meanings.

Answers: A. 1 B. 8 C. 6 D. 9 E. 5 F. 4 G. 3 H. 7 I. 2

Have students practice asking and answering questions about the notices on page 119.

4 More Real-Life Reading. Page 118.

Ask students to bring in examples of other cultural events notices and announcements from the school or local community. Students may also want to look for and print out examples from the Internet. Encourage students to share the samples that they found and talk about any new vocabulary that they learned from the reading materials.

Part 4 Personal Stories and Humor

Students can read the selections individually, in pairs, or small groups. Point out the titles of the readings and the illustrations. Have students make predications about the content based on the titles and illustrations.

1 The Excitement of a Foreign Culture. Page 120.

Have students read the first selection. As a group, summarize the reading. Then ask questions about important details. *Why does this person like to travel? Where was the person an exchange student in high school? What did the mother do every day? What were some interesting cultural customs the person learned there? What was different about the international university in Switzerland? Would you like to go to a school like that? Why or why not?*

Repeat the procedure with the other reading. Ask questions about the content or have students prepare their own questions about the readings for others in the class to answer.

Have students write about their own cross-cultural experiences. Use questions to guide them as needed. *Have you ever traveled to another country? Have you ever lived or worked with people from another cultural group? What differences did you notice? What did you like about the other culture? What didn't you like?* Encourage students to share their writing with others in the class.

2 The Humor of World Cultures. Page 121.

Read the instructions with the group. Read and discuss the jokes with the whole class or have students work in small groups to talk about their ideas. As a class, summarize the jokes or ironic situations and students' reactions to them.

Before asking students to share any jokes, you may want to have them write the jokes out first so you can screen potentially offensive ones.

Sample Answers:
Joke A: A father and son are talking in their home about a picture of the father at the Taj Mahal. The son doesn't realize it's a real palace in India. He thinks it's part of an amusement park like Disney World. The point is that Americans don't recognize many important landmarks and sites outside of their own country.

Joke B: A man from Argentina is talking to a man from Peru about mountains. They think their country has the highest and most beautiful mountains. The Peruvian tries to outdo the Argentine, but it's impossible for an echo to say anything other than the original call.

Joke C: A Scottish man is talking to his mother. He is in Australia and his mother is in Scotland. The man's neighbors seem to be in pain or have great problems, but the Scottish man is constantly playing his bagpipes. Not everyone enjoys this kind of music, so he is probably causing his neighbors' problems.

Video Activities: Chinese New Year

Before You Watch

Read the questions aloud and have students discuss their answers in groups. Have students report to the class their answers.

Watch [on video]

Ask them to read three questions. Then play the video and have them write their answers. Review the answers together.

Answers: 1. winter 2. a visitor celebrating the Chinese New Year 3. fireworks, the red lion dance

Watch Again [on video]

Have students read the statements and choices. Then replay the video and have students choose the correct items in 1 and fill in the missing words in the other items. Go over the answers.

Answers: 1. eat, see dancing, light firecrackers 2. merchants, merchant, red, money 3. the noise wards off evil spirits 4. 10

After You Watch

Read together the instructions. You may want to read aloud the sound words as clues. Have students complete the exercise and then go over the answers. Have students suggest feelings they associate with the different sounds. For example: *a baby crying: I feel worried and concerned. A boom of thunder makes me feel scared.*

Answers: 1. j 2. d 3. b 4. g 5. h 6. i 7. c 8. a 9. f 10. k 11. e

Health

Goals

- **Read about and discuss long and healthy living**
- **Understand and use outline form**
- **Use logic and reasoning**
- **Recognize meaningful connections**
- **Read about and discuss health claims**
- **Find supporting reasons**
- **Summarize**
- **Give advice and solve problems**
- **Recognize and choose word endings (suffixes)**
- **Understand instructions for health emergencies**
- **Express personal experiences and opinions**

Sample Answers:

1. The people are farmers in a small, mountainous village. They are gathering produce from a garden.

2. They probably live very simply with no running water or electricity. They probably don't have modern appliances. They probably work in the garden, prepare food, make and maintain their home and tools. They probably eat a lot of fresh produce and items they grow or produce in the village.

3. Answers will vary.

Culture Note

People who do farming and agricultural work are often viewed as backward and uneducated by those from modern, technological areas. These traditional jobs require a great deal of knowledge and understanding of nature, weather, plants, etc. There is much for modern society to learn from these people and societies.

Part 1 The Secrets of a Very Long Life

Before You Read

1 Discussing the Picture. Page 126.

Arrange students in small groups. Ask them to look at the pictures on page 126 and answer the questions. After the groups have finished their discussions, have a volunteer from each group report their responses. List vocabulary on the board. Help summarize the responses.

2 Thinking about the Answers. Page 126.

Point out the title of the reading selection "The Secrets of a Very Long Life" and the illustration on page 128. Then read the questions aloud and call on volunteers to suggest any ideas they have. Remind students that these questions will help guide them as they read the selection and work on the exercises. Point out key vocabulary: *environment, benefits, advantages, diet.* As students suggest answers, record responses and ideas on an overhead project or on a large piece of paper. Have students to develop their own pre-reading questions about the reading selection. You may want to review these questions and responses later after students have read the selection.

Sample Answers:

1. People live a long time in parts of the Himalayan Mountains, the Caucasus Mountains, and in the mountains of Ecuador.

2. The environments of these areas are clean, the climate is moderate, the water is high in minerals.

3. People eat different diets. In the Himalayans, they eat mostly raw vegetables and fruit. They seldom eat meat. In the Caucasus Mountains, they eat milk, cheese, vegetables, fruit, and meat with some red wine daily. In Ecuador, they eat mostly grain, corn, beans, potatoes, and fruit.

4. Some secrets to a long life might be natural foods, traditional herbs and medicines, less calories of food. Also the people have active lives with lots of work and exercise, less stress and worries, and extended family structures to support people.

3 Vocabulary Preview. Page 127.

As you read the words aloud, ask students to circle the ones they don't know. Encourage students to look for the words in the following reading.

Read

4 The Secrets of a Very Long Life. Page 127. [on tape/CD]

Play the tape or CD as students follow along in their books. Stop the tape or CD to ask comprehension questions and to point out key vocabulary words. Listen a second time as students read along again.

After You Read

5 Recognizing Paragraph Topics. Page 129.

Read the instructions aloud. Point out the example. Have students look back at the reading to see how the outline follows the reading

selection. Then have students complete the rest of the exercise. Go over the answers together.

Answers:

Questions:

1. Good Health of the Hunzukuts 2. Examples of their good health. Specific reasons for their good health. 3. Three. An unpolluted environment, a simple nutritious diet, physical work and activity 4. Clean air and clean water 5. Five. High in vitamins, low in fat and cholesterol, without chemicals 6. Physical work and activity

Outline:

B. The Caucasus in Russia (C)

C. Vilcabamba, Ecuador (C)

1. Hunzukut diet: raw vegetables, fruits, and *chapatis* (D)

3. Vilcabamba diet: grain, vegetables, fruit, coffee, alcohol, cigarettes (D)

2. Traditional herbs as medicines (E)

3. Fewer calories (E)

B. Stress-free (F)

C. Extended family structure (F)

A. No valid birth records (G)

Main Topic: 2

6 Understanding the Point. Page 131.

Read the instructions and have students complete the question and change the underlined words to answer the question. Then discuss the answers with the whole class.

Sample Answers: Why do people in some areas of the world live a very long time?

Study, many, long, health, physical, with, a, mountain, a steady, moderate, is important, vitamins and nutrition, fats, cholesterol, and sugar

7 Figuring Out New Vocabulary. Page 131.

After reading the instructions together, have students work in pairs to complete Exercise 7. Go over the answers with the group.

Answers:

1. Health specialists; They want other people to live long lives.; They are studying long-lived people.; C; A

2. Clean air and water and moderate temperatures; in a region; not hot and not cold; B

3. inhabitants; people; A; D

4. No; minerals; the water in the streams; D; A

5. people; C; no; valid birth records; A; yes; D

Students can look back at the reading on pages 127-128 to figure out the general meanings of other vocabulary words.

8 Recognizing Meaningful Connections. Page 134.

Read together the instructions, pointing out examples of the punctuation and phrases in the reading selection as needed. Have students complete the exercise. Go over the answers together.

Sample Answers:

1. Medical scientists and health specialists might travel to the high mountain regions to solve the mystery of a long, healthy life and to bring the secrets of longevity to the modern world.

2. The people of Hunza have good physical health because they have an unpolluted environment, a simple diet high in vitamins and nutrition, and physical work.

3. Shirali and his wife were two people similar in their longevity to the Caucasian woman Tsurba.

4. The people of the Caucasian region live well even in old age because they are almost never sick, have their own teeth, good eyesight, and a full head of hair.

5. In the environment in Vilcabamba, Ecuador, there is a clean environment, moderate climate, wind from the same direction, water high in minerals, and a region rich in flowers, fruits, vegetables, and wildlife.

6. The diets are similar because they all have natural foods without chemicals. The people use traditional herbs and medicines, and they eat fewer calories than people in other parts of the world.

7. Three other possible reasons for longevity are physical active work, less stress, and extended family structure.

8. All doctors don't believe the longevity claims because the areas don't have valid birth records and there is a natural limit to the length of the human life.

Discussing the Reading

9 Small Group Discussion. Page 136.

This activity allows students to use the vocabulary from the reading to talk about their own thoughts on longevity and becoming old. Arrange students in groups of four. Set a time limit for the small group discussions. Circulate among the groups, listening and giving assistance as needed. When all groups are finished, ask a volunteer from each group to summarize their ideas.

Answers will vary.

Part 2 Claims to Amazing Health

Before You Read

1 Vocabulary Preview. Page 137.

Read the words aloud. Students can underline words they already know and circle the ones they don't know. Tell students to look for these words in the next reading selection.

Read

2 Finding Supporting Reasons. Page 137. [on tape/CD]

Read the instructions together. Explain the difference between fact and opinion. Have students skim the paragraphs quickly and choose the best titles for the selections. Then play the tape or CD and have students follow along in their books. Stop at the end of each selection and allow students to choose the best statement of the facts and beliefs. Go over the answers.

Answers:
Paragraph Titles: A. 3 B. 1 C. 1 D. 1
Point of Facts and Beliefs: A. 1 B. 3 C. 2 D. 2

After You Read

3 Learning to Summarize. Page 140.

Read the instructions and call attention to the model outline and summary of the first paragraph. Arrange students in groups of four to complete their own outlines and summaries. You may want to assign paragraphs to the groups. Allow 10-15 minutes for groups to read and summarize their paragraphs. Have a volunteer from each group read aloud its summary. If several groups have summarized the same paragraphs, compare and contrast the different versions. Discuss any differences.

Sample Answers:
Outline B
I. A. Claims there are only two causes of disease
      2. Parasites
    B. 1. Electronic machines
      2. Herbal medicines
    C. 1. They clean the body of parasites
      2. They rebuild new healthy living cells.
II. B. Folk medicine
    C. Environmental changes
    D. Unusual therapies not available from traditional doctors.

Outline C
I. A. 1. Decreases pain of arthritis
      2. Prevent serious health disorders
    B. Foods with the color substance
      2. Blueberries, strawberries, plums
      3. Vegetables

Outline D
I. A. Part of the nucleus of every cell
    B. Determine the characteristics of living things
II. A. 2. Viruses
      3. Bacteria
    B. To find genes that cause certain diseases
    C. To prevent or repair birth defects
    D. To change gene structure
      2. To increase the length of life
    E. To change biological characteristics to benefit society
      2. Humans

Summaries will vary but should contain the important points from the outlines above.

Discussing the Reading

4 Small Group Discussion. Page 143.

Arrange students in groups of four to discuss the questions. Set a time limit of 15-20 minute. Circulate among the groups, giving assistance as needed. Ask volunteers to summarize the most interesting points discussed in their groups.

Answers will vary.

Talk It Over

Read aloud the instructions. Have students read through the choices and check the situations that interest them. You may want to have students review their answers in small groups before discussing students' responses with the whole class. Encourage students to explain what advice they would give for the situations. Students may write about their own opinion and advice column to share with the class.

Part 3 Vocabulary and Language Learning Skills

1 Recognizing Word Endings. Page 144.

After reading the instructions, call attention to the suffixes and examples in the chart. Students can complete the exercise individually. Go over the answers with the whole class. Have students suggest other words for each of the suffixes.

Answers: 2. n 3. adv. 4. adj. 5. n 6. adj. 7. adv. 8. adj. 9. adj. 10. adj. 11. adj. 12. n 13. n 14. adj. 15. adj. 16. n 17. n 18. adj. 19. n 20. adj. 21. n 22. n 23. adj. 24. adj. 25. adv. 26. adj. 27. n 28. adj. 29. adv. 30. adj

2 Choosing Word Forms with Suffixes. Page 145.

Read the instructions and have students work individually choosing the correct words in the first part. Students can then complete the chart by adding suffixes to the words as needed. Go over the answers together.

Answers: 1. longevity, various 2. scientific, physical, reason, pollution, environment 3. naturally, nutritious, beneficial, advantageous 4. usually, active, activity, movement 5. especially, available, agreement, generally 6. typical, mostly, mainly, traditional 7. important, environment, confusion, validity 8. available, information, combination, cultural 9. ignorant, medical, decisions, recommendations 10. value, genetic, defective, biological

Noun: confusion, ignorance, importance, nature, type, tradition

Adjective: available, biological, cultural, defective, famous, genetic, general, human, ignorant, important, mountainous, traditional

Adverb: actively, decisively, generally, humanly, naturally, typically

3 Real-Life Reading: Instructions for Health Emergencies. Page 147.

Read together the instructions. Then ask students to look over the emergency information on page 148 and underline words they know and circle words that they don't know. Have volunteers ask about words they circled. Invite others to suggest examples or to explain the meanings. Then have students work in pairs or small groups to answer the questions about the reading material

Sample Answers:
1. Emergency instructions
2. Cosmetics, detergents, bleaches, cleaning solutions, glue, lye, paint, turpentine, kerosene, gasoline, petroleum products, alcohol, aspirin, and other medications
3. Small children
4. TAKE ACTION Do something fast.
5. Call Poison Control
6. Poison Control Center, local emergency medical rescue squad
7. Breaking
8. Tilt back head, perform mouth to mouth breathing
9. No
10. Roll the person onto their left side, so the person doesn't choke
11. Know the emergency phone numbers, keep them near the phone
12. Answers will vary.

4 More Real-Life Reading. Page 149.

Ask students to bring in examples of other emergency or health-related reading materials. Students can look for examples on the Internet. Encourage students to share the samples that they found and talk about any new vocabulary that they learned from the reading materials. In pairs, have students practice asking and answering questions about their materials using the questions from Exercise 3 on page 149.

Part 4 Personal Stories and Humor

1 Experiences about Smoking. Page 150.
Have students to make predictions about the content based on the title and illustrations in this exercise. Have students read the selection. Then ask questions about important details. *When did this woman begin smoking? Why did she begin? Why was smoking popular? What did she learn in the book How to Stop Smoking? What finally changed her mind about smoking? Do you think she will completely give up smoking? Why or why not? How do you think her story will end?* As a group, summarize the reading.

Have students write their own opinions of smoking or other health-related situations. Use questions to guide them as needed. Encourage students to share their writing with others in the class.

2 The Humor of Health and Medicine. Page 152.
Read the first joke. Have students give their interpretations of it. Have students share experiences they have had with making doctor's appointments. Guide them as needed.

Discuss the other three jokes with the whole class or have students work in small groups to talk about their ideas. As a class, summarize the jokes and students' reactions to them.

Students can share their own humorous medical or health-related stories.

Sample Answers:
Joke A: The joke is about doctors and receptionists. They are so busy they don't really pay attention to what the patients are saying. The joke is that a doctor might charge a dead person who is dead for an appointment.

Joke B: The man in the joke may be very old, but he still has a sense of humor. The joke is his statement that a person needs to follow the rules for a hundred years to live as long as he has.

Joke C: The joke is about the office rule about recommending a doctor. The woman supposed that the receptionist meant that there are no good doctors in the office (since she can't recommend any). The receptionist was just stating a policy, not commenting on the quality of the medical care.

Video Activities: Marathon Man

Before You Watch
Arrange students in small groups. Read the questions aloud and ask students to share what they know about marathons and running in their small groups. Have students report to the class their answers.

Watch [on video]
Ask them to read the questions. Then play the video and have them write their answers. Review the answers together.

Answers: 1. He's substituting a running addiction for his alcohol addiction. 2. yes 3. to get healthy and fit

Watch Again [on video]
Have students read the questions. Then replay the video and have students fill in the correct answers. Go over the answers.

Answers: 1. 26.2 miles 2. 104 3. 200 4. 11 5. 4 hours & 45 minutes - a 10-minute mile

After You Watch

Have students research the first marathon. In small groups, students can compare and contrast the information they found.

Answers:

1. 1 & 2

2. The first marathon runner was Pheidippides, a Greek soldier. He ran from Marathon in 490 B.C. from the battlefield to Athens to tell about the Athenian victory over the Persians. He ran 22 miles without stopping. He said, "Rejoice, we conquer!" and then died.

3. A marathon is 26 miles 385 yards (42.195 km). It was set in the London Olympic Games of 1908. It was the distance from Windsor Castle to the White City stadium (26 miles) and 385 yards were added so the race would end in front of King Edward VII's royal box.

Entertainment and the Media

Goals

- **Read about and discuss the affect of visual media on people**
- **Recognize comparison and contrast**
- **Understand main idea**
- **Understand vocabulary or specific details**
- **Classify stories**
- **Arrange events in order**
- **Summarize**
- **Recognize words endings (suffixes)**
- **Identify word families**
- **Understand entertainment schedules and advertising**
- **Express personal experiences and opinions about entertainment**

Part 1 How the Visual Media Affect People

Before You Read

1 Discussing Pictures. Page 156.

Arrange students in small groups to answer the questions about the pictures on page 156. After the groups have finished their discussions, ask a volunteer from each group report the group's responses. As students describe the pictures, list vocabulary on the board. Guide students to summarize the responses. Encourage students to talk about their own feelings about the affect of media on people.

Sample Answers:
1. The people are all watching television. Two kids are fighting during an action program.
2. The people who are watching seem to feel and behave differently according to the type of program they are watching. The nature program makes the watchers quiet and calm. The action program makes some of the kids violent. The scary movie makes the girl feel nervous and afraid. The boy is pretending he is driving with the video game. The man is getting excited watching an action program. The woman is crying while watching the romantic program.

2 Thinking about the Answers. Page 157.

Point out the title of the reading selection, "How the Visual Media Affect People". Read the questions aloud and call on volunteers to suggest possible answers and to make predictions about the reading. Remind students that these questions will help guide them as they read the selection and work on the exercises. Point out key vocabulary: *media screen, negative effect, damage, low-quality programming, violent, behavior, trash TV, addiction*. Record students' responses and ideas on an overhead project or on a large piece of paper. Encourage students to develop their own pre-reading questions about the reading selection. You may want to review these questions and responses later after students have read the selection.

Answers will vary.

3 Vocabulary Preview. Page 157.

As you read the words aloud, ask students to circle the ones they don't know. Ask volunteers suggest the meanings of the new words. Tell students to look for the words as they complete the reading. Later, have students come back to this list and check their understanding of their circled words.

Read

4 How the Visual Media Affect People. Page 157. [on tape/CD]

Play the tape or CD as students follow along in their books. As needed, pause the tape or CD after every paragraph to ask comprehension questions and to point out key vocabulary words. Listen a second time as students read along again. Ask students to answer the questions about their own viewing habits. Allow students to talk about their feelings about TV and American viewing habits.

After You Read

5 Recognizing Comparison and Contrast. Page 159.

Read the instructions aloud, clarifying as needed. Be sure students understand comparison and contrast. Call attention to the outline form on page 160. Explain that the items from 1 and 2 will be used to complete the outline. Then have students work in pairs complete the rest of the exercise. Go over the answers together.

Answers:
1. I. Advantages; II. Disadvantages
2. A, A, B, C, D, A, A, E and F, G
3. Outline

I. Advantages
   A. Increase people's knowledge and thinking ability
   B. Benefit the elderly and sick
   C. Provide language learners instruction and practice
   D. Offer good entertainment for free time

II. Disadvantages
   A. Take too much time from family life and other activities
   B. Reduce people's ability to concentrate or reason
   C. Scare people or get them used to violence
   D. Cause dissatisfaction with normal life
   E. Addict people to TV and video

Some possible effects of the visual media in the lives of ordinary people around the world

6 Understanding the Point. Page 160.

Read the instructions together. Then ask students to complete the exercise. Finally, discuss the answers with the whole class.

Sample Answers:
What are some positive and negative features of visual media on ordinary people?

Positive and negative; high-quality; the average and well-educated person; can; Additionally; some; relax;

Nevertheless; separate children and their parents and decrease; harder; nightmares; crime, fights, or killing; normal or usual; dissatisfied, normal and boring; dependence; will not; easily

7 Understanding the Vocabulary of Specific Details. Page 161.

Read the instructions aloud before having students complete the exercise. Call attention to the outline of the reading materials. Be sure students understand the two steps to the exercise. Allow students to work with partners. Go over the answers with the whole class.

Answers:
1. B (IC)
2. D (IB)
3. C (IA)
4. B (ID)
5. A, C (IIB)
6. A (IIA)
7. B, A (IIC)
8. B, D, A (IID)

Discussing the Reading

8 Small Group Discussion. Page 163.

Encourage students to talk about their own thoughts and feelings about the media. Arrange students in groups of four. Set a time limit for the small group discussions. As groups talk about their answers together, circulate among the groups, listening and giving assistance as needed. When all groups are finished, ask a volunteer from each group to summarize their ideas.

Answers will vary.

Part 2 Media Stories

Before You Read

1 Vocabulary Preview. Page 164.

Read the words aloud. Students can underline words they already know circle the ones they don't know. Tell students to look for these words in the next reading selection. Students can return back to this list and check their understanding of the circled words after completing the reading selection.

Read

2 Classifying Stories and Putting Events in Order. Page 164. [on tape/CD]

Read together the instructions. Explain the purpose of skimming in this exercise-to determine the kind of story for each of the different movies. Play the tape or CD and have students classify each story and choose the best movie title or name of the TV show. Go over the answers.

Answers:

A: suspense or horror; 1. *Psycho*

B: adventure or action; 3. *Tarzan, the Ape Man*

C: science fiction; 3. *Star Trek: The Next Generation*

D: comedy; 2. *Friends*

Replay the tape or CD and have students follow along again in their books. Ask comprehension questions and point out key vocabulary words in each of the paragraphs.

After You Read

3 Learning to Summarize. Page 169.

Read the instructions together before arranging students in groups of four to practice summarizing. You may want to assign stories to the groups. Allow 10-15 minutes for groups to read and summarize their stories. Then, ask a volunteer from each group to read aloud its summary. If several groups have summarized the same stories, compare and contrast the different versions. Discuss any differences.

Sample Answers:

B. A baby boy is adopted and raised by a gorilla after his parents were killed by wild animals. A professor arrives in the jungle with his daughter, Jane, and a hunter, Clayton. They discover the apeman and find out that he is human. The apeman wants to be with the humans, but doesn't want to leave his gorilla family. The white people are captured and the apeman saves them. Jane stays with the apeman in the jungle after her father and Clayton return to England.

C. The Bynars (computerized beings) are doing the repairs on the star ship Enterprise. They order the other crew members of the Enterprise to leave the ship. Captain Picard and Riker do not leave and the star ship Enterprise disappears. The captain and Riker find the Bynars dying and asking for help. They go to the planet Bynarus to restore the data from the planet's center computer. The planet is saved and the star ship returns to the starbase.

D. Six friends (three men and three women) are friends and roommates in New York City. Chandler plans to ask Monica to marry him, so he takes her to a restaurant. Unfortunately, Monica's old boyfriend sees Monica at the restaurant, so Chandler doesn't propose to Monica. The next day, Monica's old boyfriend proposes to her. She is confused and decides to go to stay with her parents to decide. Chandler goes to her and proposes. She accepts. The other friends decide that they will all marry each other if they are still single when they are forty years old.

Discussing the Reading

4 Small Group Discussion. Page 169.

Allow 15-20 minutes for students to work in groups of four to discuss their answers to the questions. Circulate among the groups, giving assistance as needed. Ask a volunteer from each group to summarize the most interesting points discussed.

Answers will vary.

Talk It Over

Read aloud the instructions. Point out that answers may vary. Ask students to explain their reasons for their responses. Invite students to share with the class their favorites and preferences. Model expressions and phrases for talk about preferences. *I prefer ____ because. I really like _____, but I don't like _____. My favorite _____ is _____.*

Answers will vary.

Part 3 Vocabulary and Language Learning Skills

1 More Word Endings. Page 171.

After reading the instructions, go over the suffixes, meanings, and examples in the chart. You may want to have students suggest other examples of words with the suffixes. Remind students of the function of nouns, verbs, and adjectives in sentences. Have students work on the exercise in pairs or individually. Then, go over the answers with the whole class.

Answers: 1. n 2. n 3. v. 4. adj. 5. n 6. v 7. v 8. n 9. n 10. adj. 11. v 12. v

13. adj. 14. v 15. adj. 16. v 17. n 18. n 19. adj. 20. n 21. adj. 22. adj. 23. adj. 24. n 25. adj. 26. adj. 27. v 28. v 29. adj. 30. n

2 Word Families. Page 172.

Review related forms of words and the examples by reading aloud the instructions. Point out that students should note the suffixes and the placement/use of the words in the sentences as they do the exercise. Tell students to complete the exercise. Go over the answers together.

Answers: 1.prefer, concentrate 2. addicted, visual 3. criticize, violence 4. behavior, childhood 5. frequently, dissatisfied 6. envy, exciting 7. real, moral 8. truth, personalities 9. psychological, suspenseful 10. strengthens, scary

Noun: concentration, criticism, violence, children/childhood, frequency, dissatisfied, excitement, reality/realism, morality, psychology/psychologists, suspense, strength

Verb: concentrate, visualize, criticize, behave, dissatisfy, envy, realize, moralize, personalize, strengthen, scare

Adjective: addictive, visual, frequent, enviable/envious, excitable/exciting, true/truthful, personal, suspenseful, scary/scared

3 Real-Life Reading: Entertainment at Home and in the Community. Page 174.

If possible, bring in examples of entertainment schedules, calendars, and announcements. Have students suggest places where they see these real-life reading materials. Read together the instructions. Tell students to underline words they know and circle words that they don't know on the materials on page 175-176. Then arrange students in small groups to discuss the meanings of new words, to identify the subject of the real-life pieces, and to tell the general meaning or purpose of the items. Ask volunteers to summarize their groups' discussions.

Model asking questions about the community services and signs. Have volunteers answer using the information on pages 175 and 176. Tell students to work with a partner to practice asking and answering their own questions about the entertainment choices.

Answers: a. 3 b. 4 c. 1 d. 2 e. 3 f. 5 g. 6 h. 8

4 More Real-Life Reading. Page 174.

Encourage students to look for and bring in examples of other real-life reading materials related to entertainment. Students can share their samples with the class and talk about any new vocabulary that they learned.

Part 4 Personal Stories and Humor

1 Views of Entertainment in the Media. Page 177.

Have students to make predictions about the content based on the title and illustrations in the exercise. Have students read the first selection. As a group, summarize the reading. Ask questions about important details. *Does this person watch a lot of TV? What types of programs does she watch? Why does she watch and enjoy them?*

Repeat the procedure with the other two paragraphs. Have students prepare their own questions about the readings for others in the class to answer.

Have students write their own opinions about television programming. Use questions to guide them as needed. *Do you watch TV? What types of programs do you usually watch? How much time do you spend watching TV? Why?* Encourage students to share their writing with others in the class.

2 The Humor of the Entertainment Media. Page 178.

Read the instructions together. Explain that there are very few words in the pieces of humor, so it's important to look for words with multiple meanings and surprising changes. Ask students to look at the first item. Have students give their interpretations of the joke about the fighting that might occur in a family when deciding what to watch on TV.

Discuss the other one-liners with the whole class or have students work in small groups to talk about their ideas. As a class, summarize the jokes and students' reactions to them.

Students can create and share their own humorous responses.

Answers will vary.

Culture Note
- As they work, taxi drivers and barbers often talk about current events and politics with their customers. Sometimes it seems that they have the answers to solve all the problems in the country.
- During meetings, a committee or group takes notes about their discussions and decisions. These notes are called minutes.
- Many of these comedians became famous in the early days of television. Students may want to look on the Internet for information about some of these famous people or view some old movies or TV shows with these people.

Video Activities:
Quiz Shows

Before You Watch

Arrange students in small groups. Read the questions aloud and ask students to talk about their thoughts about TV shows in their small groups. Have students report to the class their answers.

Answers will vary.

Watch [on video]

Ask them to read the three questions. Remind them to think about the questions as they view the video. Allow students to discuss their answers to the questions in small groups. Then, review the answers together with the whole class.

Answers: 1. answer questions 2. They are inexpensive to produce. 3. b

Watch Again [on video]

Have students read the statements. Then replay the video and have students decide if the statements are True or False. Go over the answers.

Answers: 1. T 2. F 3. F 4. T 5. T 6. F 7. F

After You Watch

Read aloud the directions. Set a time limit for each round of the game. You may want to have groups work on the same word at the same time.

Social Life

Goals

- **Read about and discuss social relationships**
- **Recognize the structure of conversation**
- **Understand main idea**
- **Use context to complete details**
- **Make inferences**
- **Read about and discuss the "perfect mate"**
- **Summarize**
- **Recognize negative prefixes**
- **Understand personal ads**
- **Express personal experiences and opinions**

Part 1 Meeting the Perfect Mate

Before You Read

1 Discussing Pictures. Page 182.
Point out the eight pictures and ask students to describe the people and their expressions. Have students read what each person is saying. Read the questions aloud and call on volunteers to answer. Encourage students to talk about the different ways to meet boyfriends/girlfriends. List vocabulary on the board.

Answers will vary.

2 Thinking about the Answers. Page 182.
Read the questions aloud and call on volunteers to suggest possible answers. Point out key vocabulary: *marriage, boyfriend, girlfriend, meeting people*. As students suggest answers,

record students' responses and ideas on an overhead project or on a large piece of paper. You may want to review these responses later after students have read the selection.

Sample Answers:
1. A common kind of marriage in Korea in the past was an arranged marriage where the parents chose the mate for their child.
2. Young people around the world meet people through friends, going out to dances and parties, at school or work, at clubs, and on the Internet.
3. Answers will vary.

3 Vocabulary Preview. Page 183.
Read the words aloud and have students circle the ones they don't know. Students can look for the words they don't know in the reading. Have students check their understanding of the circled words after they complete the reading selection.

Read

4 Meeting the Perfect Mate. Page 183.
Play the tape as students follow along in their books. You may want to stop the tape after every paragraph to check understanding and point out vocabulary words. Listen a second time as students read along.

After You Read

5 Recognizing the Structure of Conversations. Page 184.
Read the instructions together. Point out the outline form on page 185 that students will complete. Have students look back at the reading on pages 183 and 184 to guide them as they complete the outline. Go over the answers together.

Answers:

I. Introduction: reasons for interviewing people

    A. I'm studying "Social Structure" in a graduate seminar.

    B. I'm interviewing people about ways to meet potential mates.

II. Arranged marriages

    A. Mates may meet for the first time on their wedding day.

    B. Husbands and wives may learn to love each other.

III. Meeting people in dance clubs

    A. You can talk or just listen to music.

    B. The women act unfriendly because a lot of men are too aggressive

IV. Finding friends in cyberspace

    A. You can go online at home, in cafes, and in other places.

    B. You don't know what is unreal or dangerous about people you meet on the Web.

V. Meeting in health clubs or the gym

    A. People with common interest in physical exercise meet here.

    B. If you're not really interested in exercise, there might be a problem.

There are <u>advantages</u> and disadvantages to the various ways of <u>meeting potential mates</u>.

6 Understanding the Main Idea. Page 185.
After reading the instructions, have students change the underlined words and phrases to complete the summary of the reading selection. Have students explain the reasons for their answers.

Answers:
Ex. advantages and disadvantages; mates;

1. A disadvantage; love each other
2. dance; women; a lot of men
3. convenient; everywhere; difficult
4. something in common; loses interest

7 Supplying Left-Out Words and References. Page 186.
Read together the instructions. Have students work individually in pairs to complete the statements with the missing words. Go over answers with the group.

Answers:
1. For meeting a possible mate
2. Match; can you match
3. Of arranged marriages
4. They were upset
5. Women; to nightclubs

In the second part of the exercise, point out that students will identify the idea to which the underlined words refer. Go over the example and clarify as needed. Then have students complete this part of the exercise. Review the answers with the class.

Answers:
1. Seminar
2. Matched marriage
3. Their children's
4. Meet
5. Dance clubs seem great.
6. In cyberspace
7. The healthy atmosphere in the gym is continuing into the relationship. The idea sounds wonderful.
8. I hate to exercise.

You may want to arrange students in pairs to practice asking and answering the questions about references to previous ideas. Call attention to the sample question in the Example on page 187.

Finally, have students complete the answers to the questions on page 182. Go over the answers with the group. Discuss any differences in the responses.

Sample Answers:
1. A common kind of marriage in Korea in the past was an arranged marriage where the parents chose the mate for their child.
2. Young people around the world meet people through friends, going out to dances and parties, at school or work, at clubs, on the Internet.
3. Answers will vary.

Discussing the Reading

8 Small Group Discussion. Page 188.
Arrange students in groups of four. Give the groups about 15-20 minutes to discuss the questions. Circulate among the groups, listening and giving assistance as needed. When all groups are finished, ask reporters from each group to share the most interesting information form their groups.

Answers will vary.

Part 2 Meeting the Perfect Mate (continued)

Before You Read

1 Vocabulary Preview. Page 188.
Read the words aloud and have students circle the ones they don't know. Encourage students to explain the meanings of the words they do know. After reading the selection, have students look back at the vocabulary words to check again their understanding. Students can use context

clues from the reading or look up the meanings of the words in a dictionary.

Read

2 Making Inferences. Page 188.
Read together the instructions and review the purpose of skimming in this exercise-to read for literal meaning. Students will re-read the selection later for details. Play the tape and have students read along for the basic meaning of the material. Then replay the tape and tell students to read again to gain a better understanding of the selection. Ask comprehension questions and point out key vocabulary words in each of the paragraphs.

After You Read

3 Identify Inferred and Stated Ideas. Page 190.
Review the meaning of *infer*. Read the instructions together clarifying as needed. Students can work in pairs to complete the exercise. Then go over the answers. Discuss any differences and have volunteers point out lines and information from their reading that supports their answers.

Answers:
1. X 2. O 3. X 4. X 5. O 6. O 7. O
8. X 9. O 10. O 11. X 12. X 13. O 14. O
15. X 16. X

4 Learning to Summarize. Page 190.
After reading the instructions together, arrange students in groups of four to answer the questions and prepare their summary of the reading selection. Encourage students to look back at the selection as they work. Ask a volunteer from each group to share the summary. Discuss any variations in the summaries.

Sample Answers:

1. sometimes meet each other on their wedding days and are chosen by the parents or grandparents.

2. the environment is exciting and you can go just to dance or listen to music.; The women are unfriendly and cold and men are too aggressive

3. you don't know what is real and what isn't real.

4. people have interests in common; the person doesn't really have that interest

5. you have a lot in common with the people you meet; are too general in your answers; find match for you

6. you film yourself and view videos about other people; many people

7. you can make small talk which might lead to a date

8. that maybe a matched marriage is not a bad idea

Discussing the Reading

5 Small Group Discussion. Page 192.

Encourage students to refer back to the reading and vocabulary list for useful words and expressions as they discuss their answers to the questions. Allow 15-20 minutes to discuss the questions. As groups work, go around the room to listening and give assistance as needed. When all groups are finished, invite students to share the most interesting information from their groups.

Talk It Over

This activity gives students a chance to discuss some common proverbs about love. Read together the instructions. Have students complete the matching exercise first and go over the answers. Then arrange students in groups of four to talk whether they agree or disagree with the proverbs. Allow 15-20 minutes for discussion.

Answers: 1. c 2. a 3. b 4. d 5. e 6. i 7. f 8. g 9. h 10. j

Part 3 Vocabulary and Language Learning Skills

1 Recognizing Negative Prefixes. Page 193.

Read together the instructions. Point out that prefixes are added to the beginning of words. Go over the examples with the class. Remind students that there are some words that begin with the same letters as a prefix, but they are not really prefixes and root words. For example: *important*. Ask students to complete the exercise in pairs. Then discuss the answers with the whole class. Students may look in a dictionary for meanings as needed.

Answers:

1. X 2. <u>dis</u>ease 3. <u>dis</u>honesty 4. <u>dis</u>respect
5. X 6. <u>il</u>legal 7. <u>il</u>logical 8. X 9. X 10. X
11. <u>im</u>moral 12. <u>im</u>mortality 13. <u>im</u>patience
14. <u>im</u>polite 15. <u>in</u>ability 16. <u>in</u>dependence
17. <u>in</u>directness 18. X 19. X 20. <u>in</u>formal
21. X 22. <u>non</u>sense 23. <u>non</u>traditional
24. <u>non</u>-Western 25. X 26. X 27. <u>un</u>limited
28. <u>un</u>related 29. <u>un</u>usually 30. <u>un</u>welcome

1. dis 2. dis 3. il 4. im 5. im 6. in 7. in
8. non 9. non 10. un 11. un 12. un 13. un
14. un 15. un

2 Using Opposites. Page 194.

Read the instructions and go over the examples. Point out that by adding or deleting prefixes you can create words with opposite meanings. Have students work individually on the exercise. Go over the answers.

Answers: possible, natural, easy, friendly, happy, unpackaged, natural, fast, like, low, different, capable, unmarried (single), like, convenient, helpful, disadvantages, few, successful

**3 Real-Life Reading: Personal Ads.
Page 195.**

Read together the instructions. You may want to bring in some examples of personal ads from local papers and magazines. Remind students to use context clues to guess meanings of new words.

Then ask students to look over the ads and try to match the men and the women. They can underline words they know and circle words that they don't know. Have volunteers ask about words they circled. Invite others to suggest definitions or to explain the meanings. Students can describe the different people in the ads.

Answers will vary. Possibilities: 1. A.   5. E.

4 More Real-Life Reading. Page 196.

Ask students to do this as a homework assignment. Students can look for dating services and personal on the Internet, too. Allow time for students to share the samples that they found and talk about vocabulary that they learned from the reading materials.

Part 4 Personal Stories and Humor

1 The Beginning of a Friendship. Page 196.

Have students read the selection. As a group, summarize it. Ask questions about important details. *Who is Lucy? Where did her family move from? Do the children in the class seem friendly to Lucy? What do they do? Why didn't Lucy go play with the other children during recess? Why didn't Lucy talk to the other children? Why do you think Lucy didn't want to go back to school the next day? Was her day any different? How*

do you know that Lucy was very sad? What do you think about the children who laughed at her? Who is Henry? When did he arrive in the school? Where does he sit in class? Does Henry act the same as the other children? What does he do? Is it easy or difficult for you to make new friends? Why? What advice would you give to Lucy?

Have students write their own opinions of friendship and making friends in the United States. Use questions to guide them as needed. *How can you meet new people? Do you think Americans are friendly or unfriendly? Why? How did you meet your best friend? Where and when did you meet? Why is your friendship special?* Encourage students to share their writing with others in the class.

2 The Humor of Social Life and Love. Page 198.

Read together the instructions. Have students look back on page 192 for some samples of proverbs. Students can match the originals with the new comical versions. Guide students as they discuss the humor in the new versions.

Answers:
- Love makes the world go 'round.
- Absence makes the heart grow fonder.
- All's fair in love and war.
- Better to love and lose than never to love at all.
- Love is blind.
- Any friend of yours is a friend of mine.
- A friend in need is a friend indeed.
- The best of friends must part.
- A woman without a man is like a fish without water.
- The course of true love never did run smooth.

Video Activities: Online Dating

Before You Watch

Read the questions aloud and ask students to discuss their answers in small groups. Have students report to the class their answers.

Answers will vary.

Watch [on video]

Ask them to read the events. Then play the video and have them number the events in proper order. Review the answers together.

Answers: 2, 5, 1, 4, 3

Watch Again [on video]

Have students read the discussion questions. Replay the video and have students talk about their answers in groups. Ask a volunteer in each group to report the group's responses.

Possible Answers:

1. She meant that she wasn't ugly.

2. Because they me in an anonymous setting - an Internet chat room.

3. 2 weeks

4. 6 months

5. that it wouldn't last

6. Patrick says she's his princess. Vesna says he's her soulmate.

7. an online dating service that they started

After You Watch

You may want to have students find and read ads for homework. Later in class, arrange students in groups of four to share their findings and answer the questions. Have a volunteer from each group report their ideas.

Answers will vary.

Customs, Celebrations, and Holidays

Goals

- **Read about and discuss dinner etiquette**
- **Recognize question-and-answer letter form**
- **Understand main idea**
- **Use context clues**
- **Make inferences**
- **Read about and discuss holiday traditions**
- **Summarize**
- **Recognize prefixes, stems, suffixes**
- **Understand announcements and greeting cards**
- **Express personal experiences and opinions**

Part 1 A Dinner Party

Before You Read

1 Discussing the Picture. Page 202.

Ask students to identify the place, objects on the table, and the feelings of the young man. Have students suggest reasons for a large formal dinner. Then read the questions aloud and call on volunteers to answer. Encourage students to talk about things that are the same and things that are different from the pictures and their own formal dinner customs. Make a list of vocabulary on the board as students describe the picture.

Sample Answers:

1. The young man is at a formal dining table. It might be in a home or in a restaurant. He looks quite worried and

confused. He's looking up and asking for help.

2. He's confused about all the different utensils at the place settings. He probably doesn't know which utensils to use or what to do first at the table.

3. I think he should act more relaxed and watch what the other people do and act the way they do.

4. I've had a problem like this when I visited the family of an American friend. I sat next to my friend and asked him what to do.

2 Thinking about the Answers. Page 202.

Have students glance at the reading selection on pages 203-204. Point out the different letters. Then, call on volunteers to suggest answers to the pre-reading questions. As students suggest answers, record students' responses and ideas on an overhead project or on a large piece of paper. You may want to review these responses later after students have read the selection.

Sample Answers:

1. The people who wrote the letters are probably going to or giving a dinner party. They're writing to "Etty Kitt," who is a person who gives advice on manners and proper etiquette.

2. You should bring something to someone's house for dinner, such as some flowers or a bottle of wine.

3. You should arrive for a dinner party on time or just a few minutes later (5-10 minutes).

4. If you don't know which knife, fork, or spoon to use at a formal dinner party, watch what other people are using or ask someone.

5. If you give a dinner party, you can help your guests feel comfortable by spending time with them and by providing some snacks and drinks before the meal so guests can talk and relax. You should act

naturally toward them and to treat them as you would like to be treated.

6. Some secrets of a successful dinner party are to spend time with your guests, to serve snacks and drinks, and to act naturally.

3 Vocabulary Preview. Page 203.

Tell students to go through the lists and circle words they know. Then read the words aloud and have volunteers explain or define the ones they know. Remind students to look for the words as they complete the reading exercises. After they have completed the reading selections, tell students to look back and check their understanding of the circled words.

Read

4 A Dinner Party. Page 203. [on tape/CD]

Play the tape or CD as students follow along in their books. Stop the tape or CD occasionally to check students' understanding and to point out vocabulary words. Listen a second time.

After You Read

5 Recognizing Question-and-Answer Letter Form. Page 204.

Read the instructions about the organization of topics. Have students identify who wrote the letters and received answers. Go over the answers.

Answers: Organization of Topics: 1. guest 2. guest 3. host 4. host

Then have students indicate the letter where each idea is found. Go over the answers together, asking students to find the sentence(s) as needed.

Answers: Ideas from the Reading: 1. B 2. B 3. A 4. C 5. D 6. A 7. A 8. D 9. A 10. D 11. B 12. B

Finally, have students choose the main idea. Encourage students to explain their reasons for their choice.

Answer: Main Idea of the Reading: 4.

6 Understanding the Main Idea. Page 205.

Read the instructions carefully together. Be sure that students understand the difference between "fact" and "opinion." Point out that facts can be true or false. Opinions are statements of personal belief or feeling. You may want to have students read through the statements in the exercise and identify which ones are facts and which ones are opinions. Then, have students decide if the statements of facts are true or false and make corrections for the false statements. Then discuss the answers with the whole class.

Answers:
1. T
2. O
3. F Dinner guests should always bring a small gift to the hosts of the party
4. F Arriving at a party on time or a little late is very important; call the hosts if you are running late.
5. T
6. F In most cultures, party guests are expected to express thanks or appreciation for their hosts' hospitality.
7. F When you give a party, you should spend as much time as possible with your visitors.
8. O
9. F Because it's important for both guests and hosts to feel comfortable, everyone should try to be polite.
10. O

7 Supplying Missing Information. Page 206.

Read together the instructions. Have students work individually or in pairs to complete the sentences in Exercise 7. Go over the answers with the group.

Sample Answers:

1. The dinner; the visit; the dinner (occasion); nervous

2. a gift; early; utensils; show appreciation

3. appropriate; arrival; will be late

4. be uncomfortable; thank them; will be appreciated

5. a successful party

6. lets you spend time with your visitors; makes them feel more comfortable; talk; can help themselves; they can sit and talk with different people

7. good hospitality; act naturally toward them

Discussing the Reading

8 Small Group Discussion. Page 208.

Arrange students in groups of four to discuss their ideas. Give the groups about 15-20 minutes to discuss the questions. Circulate among the groups, listening and giving assistance as needed. When all groups are finished, ask a volunteer from each group to share the most interesting information from their groups.

Answers will vary.

Part 2 A Traditional Holiday

Before You Read

1 Vocabulary Preview. Page 208.

Read the words aloud and have students circle the ones they don't know. Encourage students to explain the meanings of the words they do know. Students may want to come back to this vocabulary section after reading the selection to check again their understanding of the circled words.

Read

2 Making Inferences. Page 208. [on tape/CD]

Read together the instructions. Then play the tape or CD as students follow along in their books. Stop the tape or CD after every paragraph and have students complete the title for the paragraph. Then replay the tape as students read along in their books again. Stop again after each paragraph and ask students to identify the main idea. You may also want to check understanding and point out vocabulary words in each of the paragraphs.

Answers:
Titles:
B. A Mixture of Customs   C. Witches: A Symbol of Halloween   D. Halloween in North America   E. Halloween in Latin American Culture

Main Ideas:
A. The celebration began...   B. ...the Romans, Christians, and Celts.   C. There are many beliefs...   D. ... a children's holiday with costumes and candy.   E. ... is a holiday to welcome back the souls.

After You Read

3 Making Inferences. Page 210.

Review making inferences. Read and clarify the instructions as needed before asking students to complete the exercise. As you go over the answers with the group, have volunteers point out references in the readings for the stated and implied statements.

Answers: 1. X 2. O 3. X 4. O 5. O 6. X 7. O 8. O 9. X 10. O 11. O 12. X 13. O 14. X

4 Learning to Summarize. Page 211.

Review what a summary is. Read the instructions and call attention to the paraphrases of the important vocabulary. Arrange students in groups of five to summarize assigned paragraphs. Remind groups that the topic sentence gives the main idea of a paragraph and the other sentences give details. Allow 10-15 minutes for groups to prepare their summaries. Have a volunteer from each group read aloud its summary. If several groups have summarized the same paragraphs, compare and contrast the versions. Discuss any differences.

Sample Answers:

A   The celebration of Halloween began in the Celtic culture centuries ago in areas of France and the British Isles. It was a festival at the beginning of winter. They believed that the Lord of the Dead called back the ghosts of the dead people on October 31. People wanted to chase away the bad ghosts, so they made big fires.

B   Through the centuries, Halloween added customs from the Romans, Christians, and Celts. The Romans had a celebration at the end of harvest time. Christians had a religious holiday on November 1 to remember good people in their religion. The day before the holy day became "the holy evening" or All Hallow's Eve.

C   There are many beliefs associated with witches, a common symbol of Halloween. In Britain, people believed that these old wise women could tell the future and use magic words. Others thought that witches had special meetings and could fly on brooms. Some Christians wanted to stop witches and the belief in witches.

D   Today in North American, Halloween is a children's holiday with costumes and candy. Children dress up like ghosts, witches, and devils. They go to houses and say "Trick or treat!" They receive candy, apples, or other things from the people in the houses.

E   In contrast to Halloween, the Days of the Dead is a holiday to welcome back the souls of dead relatives. It's not a scary or sad holiday in Latin American culture. It's held on November 1 and 2. People honor the dead by getting together at the graves, lighting candles, having picnics, making music, and telling stories.

Discussing the Reading

5   Small Group Discussion. Page 211.
Arrange students in groups of four or five to discuss their answers to the questions. Encourage students to refer back to the reading and vocabulary list for useful words and expressions. Give the groups about 15-20 minutes to discuss the questions. Circulate among the groups, listening and giving assistance as needed. When all groups are finished, invite students to share the most interesting information from their groups.

Talk It Over

Read together the instructions and questions. Allow time for students to complete the matching exercise individually. Then arrange students in groups of four or five to compare their answers and explain the reasons and describe any personal experiences they have with the holiday or a similar holiday celebration in their own culture. Allow 15-20 minutes for discussion. You may want to have groups report their findings.

Answers: 1. B 2. F 3. D 4. A 5. H 6. C 7. E 8. G

Part 3 Vocabulary and Language Learning Skills

1   Recognizing Other Prefixes. Page 213.
Read together the instructions to about prefixes. Have students suggest words that begin with the previously learned prefixes: dis-, il-, im-, in-, non-, and un-. Read the examples of words with the new prefixes. Encourage volunteers to define the words to show the meaning of the prefix. Then have students match the words with their meanings. Students can work individually or in pairs on the three sets of exercises. Go over the answers together.

Answers:

A. Words with Similar Meanings:
   1. c 2. e 3. g 4. a 5. b 6. k 7. d 8. l
   9. i 10. j 11. h 12. f

B. Words With Opposite Meanings:
   1. e 2. h 3. a 4. f 5. k 6. j 7 b 8. c
   9. l 10. g 11. d 12. i

C. 1. considered, happy, event, new,
      universally, turn, replace

   2. contained, introduced, improved,
      included, additional, observed

   3. different, appearance, serious, religious,
      exchange, presents, frequent, exciting

2 Recognizing Prefixes, Stems, and Suffixes. Page 215.

Read the instructions and go over examples of
suffixes, prefixes, and stems. Have students work
individually on the exercise. Go over the answers
together. Ask volunteers to identify the prefixes
and suffixes in the words and explain the
meanings.

Answers:

1. communities, public, protect, unlucky,
   brightness, represent, happiness,
   enlightenment

2. completely, rearrange, renewal, singers,
   instruments, disguised, costumes,
   symbolizes

3. rebirth, observance, consistent, symbolic,
   ancient, environment, relighting,
   disruption

3 Real-Life Reading: Announcement and Greeting Cards. Page 217.

Read together the instructions and talk about the
kinds of cards. Then ask students to classify the
cards on pages 218-219. They can underline
words they know and circle words that they
don't know. As you go over the answers, have
volunteers ask about words they circled. Invite
others to suggest definitions or to explain the
meanings. Students can talk about any

experiences they have had sending or receiving
cards and announcements.

Answers: 1. j 2. a 3. f 4. b 5. g 6. i
7. l 8. m

4 More Real-Life Reading. Page 220.

Encourage students to look for and bring in
information and examples of reading materials
related to holidays and celebrations in the local
area. Allow time for students to share the samples
that they found and talk about vocabulary that
they learned from the reading materials. If
appropriate, you may want to have take a class
trip to participate in or observe a local holiday
celebration or event.

Part 4 Personal Stories and Humor

This part of the chapter provides lighter reading.
Students can read the selections individually, in pairs,
or small groups. Point out the titles of the reading and
the illustrations. Have students make predications
about the content based on the titles and illustrations.

1 The Spirit of the Holiday Season. Page 220.

Have students read the first selection. As a group,
summarize the reading. Then ask questions about
important details. *What holiday is this about?
What does the sign say in the picture? Who was
out shopping? What was the grandmother
looking at? Was the man polite or rude to the
grandmother? How do you know? What didn't
he like about the clerk? When did the woman
see the man again? Was he more polite this
time? Why did the woman throw him out of the
store? Why is the story called "The Spirit of the
Holiday Season"?*

Repeat the procedure with the other selection.
Ask questions about the content or have students
prepare their own questions about the reading
for others in the class to answer.

Have students write their own views on holiday spirit. Use questions to guide them as needed. Do you like holidays? Why or why not? How do you feel before and on holidays? Why? Does everyone like holidays? What would the perfect holiday be like for you? Encourage students to share their writing with others in the class.

2 The Humor of Celebrations and Holidays. Page 222.

Read together the instructions. As needed, clarify the meaning of "punch-line." You may want to bring in some samples of humorous greeting cards. Then have students complete the exercise by matching the cover and interior messages. Discuss the answers together.

Answers:

1. • Being a Dad meant years of hard work, major responsibilities, and endless sacrifice, but look what you've got in return.... on second thought, may you shouldn't think too much about that HAPPY FATHER'S DAY from your "GROAN" CHILDREN

    • TO MY SISTER, Because it's your birthday, I want to tell you how I really feel. I feel just fine, thanks.

    • The Christmas season came and went... and still no cards has this family sent. So please accept our sentiments on this Day of Presidents (February).

    • I LOVE YOU, I LOVE YOU, I LOVE YOU, I LOVE YOU... If you had to look inside this Valentine's Day card to see who sent it, we're in serious trouble. Your hubby forever.

    • Happy Valentine's Day to my favorite sister... So what if you're my only sister?

    • Another birthday? Because we are mature, reasonable, sophisticated people, there is only one thing to say. You're older than I am, you're older than I am, nyah-nyah, nyah, nyah-nyah.

    • Happy Mother's Day, MOM! I know you've thought of it a few times,... but thanks for not running away!

    • Pecsa, my pet codfish, and I want you to get well soon! You've heard of a get-well cod, haven't you?

2. • Father's Day; from children (grown/adult); to father

    • Birthday; from sibling (brother or sister); to sister

    • Presidents' Days; from a family; to friends or relatives

    • Valentine's Day; from husband; to wife

    • Valentine's Day; from sibling (brother or sister); to sister

    • Birthday; from friend or relative; to friend or relative

    • Mother's Day; from son or daughter; to mother

    • Get Well card; from friend or relative; to friend or relative

3. • The joke is the "groan" (grown) children. The father went through a lot of hard work parenting (so he "groaned" a lot) as his children were growing. Now they are grown.

    • The joke is that the brother or sister tells how he or she is feeling right now, not about his or her feelings about the sister.

    • The joke is about sending out cards too late. This message rhymes!

    • The joke is making fun of relationships between husband and wife. If the wife doesn't know who loves her, there is a problem!

    • This is about relationships between siblings.

    • In this joke, the first part is about how mature and adult the two people are, and the second part shows that they are still really like little kids.

    • The point of this card is about the hard work of parenting.

- The point of this card is a word joke between "card" and "cod" which sound a little bit alike.
4. and 5. Answers will vary.

Students can create their own cards or visit a local card shop to read and write down other examples of humorous cards.

Video Activities: Puerto-Rican Day Parade

Before You Watch
Read the questions aloud and ask students to discuss their answers in small groups. Have students report to the class their answers.

Sample Answers:
1. A parade is a procession of people often with music and costumes.
2. You can often see bands playing music, groups or clubs in uniforms, cars, floats, flags, horses, clowns, etc.
3. Puerto Rico is an island in the Caribbean. It's capital is San Juan. The people speak Spanish and study English in school. Puerto Rico is a commonwealth of the United States, so its people are American citizens. They use American money, etc. The climate is tropical. They produce sugar cane, citrus fruits, coffee. Many Puerto Ricans also live in the continental United States.

Watch [on video]
Ask them to read questions. Then play the video and have them write their answers. Review the answers together.

Answers:
1. the 500th anniversary of Columbus's discovery of Puerto Rico
2. spectators, a queen, a marching band, flag wavers, floats, police, the mayor of New York

Watch Again [on video]
Have students read the four statements. Then replay the video and have students fill in the missing words. Go over the answers.

Answers: 1. 500 2. proud 3. salsa 4. 20,000

After You Watch
Read together the about words that are used as both nouns and verbs. Then have students complete the questions. Go over the answers together.

Answers:
1. float—noun, respect—noun, estimate—verb
2. Answers will vary. Samples:

The rock did not <u>float</u> on the water, but the leaf did float.

I loved the rainbow <u>float</u> in the parade. It was made of flowers and feathers.

People need to <u>respect</u> and be polite to each other.

The people watching the parade saluted in <u>respect</u> to the flag.

We tried to <u>estimate</u> the number of people marching in the parade.

The <u>estimate</u> was more than 5,000.

Science and Technology

Goals

- **Read about and discuss uses of technology**
- **Organize information in an outline**
- **Understand main idea**
- **Use punctuation clues**
- **Read about and discuss controversial issues in technology**
- **Make inferences**
- **Summarize**
- **Understand word use in context**
- **Understand technology instructions**
- **Express personal experiences and opinions**

Part 1 Everyday Uses of Technology

Before You Read

1 Discussing Pictures. Page 226.

Arrange students in small groups. Ask them to look at the pictures on page 226 and answer the questions. After the groups have finished their discussions, have a volunteer from each group report their responses. List vocabulary on the board as students describe the pictures. Help summarize the responses. Encourage students to identify places where they have seen these symbols or might see them.

Sample Answers:

1. Atomic energy; mechanics, chemistry, electricity, communications, biology, mathematics, radiation, telecommunications, medicine, computer, engineering (physics)
2. Answers will vary.

2 Thinking about the Answers. Page 226.

Point out the title of the reading selection "Everyday Uses of Technology" and the illustrations on page 226. Then read the questions aloud and call on volunteers to suggest any ideas they have. Remind students that these questions will help guide them as they read the selection and work on the exercises. Point out key vocabulary: *controversial, issues, technology, computer, communicate, computer technology, medical technology, advances.* As students suggest answers, record students' responses and ideas on an overhead project or on a large piece of paper. Encourage students to develop their own pre-reading questions about the reading selection. You may want to review these questions and responses later after students have read the selection.

Sample Answers:

1. Some controversial issues are: genetic engineering, cloning, nuclear energy, mass media, high-tech medical treatments.
2. Computers can improve someone's social life and ability to communicate because they do not need to speak directly to a person. It can be done through a computer. You can contact more people throughout the world.
3. In the home, computer technology can be found in microwave oven programs, stoves, and other appliances, entertainment equipment, and even in cars.
4. Medical technology has advanced with computers to maintain and send patient information, sensors for diagnosing and

monitoring patients in emergency situations, machines for CAT scans and DSA scans, machines for sonography, thermography, and lasers.

3 Vocabulary Preview. Page 226.

As you read the words aloud, ask students to circle the ones they don't know. You may want to have volunteers suggest the meanings of the new words. Encourage students to look for the words in the following reading. After completing the reading selection, have students come back to this list and check their understanding of the circled words.

Read

4 Everyday Uses of Technology. Page 227. [on tape/CD]

Play the tape or CD as students follow along in their books. You may want to stop the tape or CD after paragraphs to ask comprehension questions and to point out key vocabulary words. Listen a second time as students read along.

After You Read

5 Review of Outline Organization. Page 228.

Read the instructions aloud. Review the purpose, organization, and divisions of an outline. Then have students complete the outline using words and information from the reading selection. Students should then select the best statement of the main idea of the reading selection. Go over the answers together.

Answers:

I. A. 1. In homes
   B. 2. Use to look for potential dates or mates
      a. personal ads with photos on screen
      c. on-line video connections

II. A. 1. Person writes message and sends it
      2. computer dials server (central computer than collects and distributes electronic information
   B. Advantage: messages sent in a few seconds

III. A. 1. a. microwave oven
        c. dishwasher
        d. washing machine and dryer

III. A. 2. b. Televisions
        c. VCRs
     4. Family microcomputer

IV. Computers in medical sciences
   A. Computer use in ambulance by EMTs
      3. Technicians get advice on how to keep patient alive
   B. Doctors use to examine body
      2. b. Temperature (thermography)
        c. Radio waves
        d. Radio-active tracers
      3. Surgical procedures
        a. Cameras and lasers for heart surgery

Main idea of reading: 1

6 Understanding the Main Idea. Page 230.

Read the instructions. Review the difference between implied statements (inferences) and direct statements and talk about how writers may use them both. Then ask students to complete the exercise by identifying items that the writer stated or suggested and those items that the writer did not say or imply. Then discuss the answers with the whole class. Ask volunteers to point out parts of the reading that support their responses.

Answers: 1. O 2. X 3. X 4. O 5. X 6. O

7 Special Uses of Punctuation. Page 230.

After reading the instructions together, have students look for other examples of the punctuation and italics in the reading selection. Tell students to work individually to write the words or phrases to complete the sentences in Exercise 7. Go over the answers with the group.

Answers:

2. "Electronic bulletin board": a place for posting electronic messages

    "Chat room": a place where people can meet and talk through the computer

    Computer uses can put messages for others to read and read other people's messages. They can also talk to many different people about topics of interest to them.

3. "Personals": ads that people place on the computer.

    "Digitized video segments": electronic forms of motion pictures.

    "Live online video connections": movie connections that are broadcast through computers.

    Computer uses might "meet" in nontraditional ways because they will not meet face-to-face or speak person-to-person. They can meet even though they are thousands of miles away from each other.

4. "E-mail": electronic mail-letters and messages.

    "Servers": receive and give out information.

    Computers "deliver" information from senders to receivers because the computer collects the information from the senders and stores and distributes the information to the receiver.

5. "Computer chips": small pieces of computer parts.

    "Program": a person gives a plan to a computer-he or she teaches the computer to do something.

    A household that is "programmed" with "computer chips" might begin making the coffee at a particular time, cooking a meal at a set time, washing dishes,

washing and drying clothes. The machines would be programmed to begin their tasks at specific times.

6. "Sensors": things to read feelings.

    "Slice through": CAT and DSA take pictures that are cross-sections of the body and organs. They can take a view straight through as a knife would cut.

    "Surgical procedure": a way of doing something in surgery.

    Science is advancing in medical investigation and healthcare through the use of sensors to record how a patient is feeling and parts of the boy operating. Doctors can use machines to see the inside of organs and to identify exactly where a problem might be. They have many surgical procedures that don't require cutting into the body, so these procedures are safer and don't create other problems.

7. "Interactive media": This means that the media has an effect on the viewer or listener. The people will respond to the media.

    "Genetic engineering": designing and building genes.

    "High-tech" equipment: tools, machines, and appliances that use high technology (computers).

    Some controversial issues and questions raised by "interactive media" are privacy, the controlling of minds, changing family life and personal relationships. In "genetic engineering", there questions about the effect the new genetically-changed foods on people's health. There are questions about whether high-tech medical treatments will also be able to improve the health and happiness of people's lives along with letting them live for a longer time.

Discussing the Reading

8 Small Group Discussion. Page 233.

This activity allows students to use the vocabulary from the reading to talk about their own opinions and concerns about technology and science. Arrange students in groups of four. Set a time limit for the small group discussions. As groups talk about their answers together, circulate among the groups, listening and giving assistance as needed. When all groups are finished, ask a volunteer from each group to summarize their ideas.

Answers will vary.

Part 2 Controversial Issues in Technology

Before You Read

1 Vocabulary Preview. Page 234.

Read the words aloud. Students can underline words they already know and circle the ones they don't know. Tell students to look for these words in the next reading selection. Students can return back to this list and check their understanding of the circled words after completing the reading selection.

Read

**2 Making Inferences. Page 234.
[on tape/CD]**

Review together the instructions before students listen to the tape or CD. Students should read along in the books and then choose the best title for each selection. Then replay the tape or CD and have students read along for details. Allow time for students to answer the questions after each selection. Go over the answers.

Answers:

Titles of Paragraphs: 4, 3, 2, 1

Sample Answers about Paragraphs:

What's Mine is Mine
1. The paragraph is about laws on privacy of e-mail at work.
2. A person has a secret password for his or her e-mail.
   E-mail systems are monitored and watched.
3. The main idea of the paragraph is that employees can have his or her own e-mail at work, but the employers can have lists of the passwords for monitoring e-mail systems.

Surveying the Surveillance Issues
1. It's about high-tech surveillance systems.
2. They might complain that the systems cause employee stress and invades people's privacy.
3. Electronic surveillance can be used for good and bad-to solve crimes or to watch employees at work.

Electronic Mysteries in the Sky
1. Mysterious electronic interference with airline communication systems.
2. Portable computers, CD players, electronic games, etc. might cause the problems.
3. Entertainment equipment might cause airplane electronic communication problems.

Attack of the Killer Tomatoes?
1. It's about genetically altered foods and plants.
2. People are worried if these things are safe for people to eat.
3. Biotechnology creates new foods that are better in some ways but may be unsafe.

After You Read

3 Identifying What the Writer Said. Page 237.

Read the instructions. Remind students that a write often implies information. Have students complete the exercise marking the ideas that were in the selection and those that were not. As you go over the answers together, have volunteers show places in the reading that support their responses.

Answers: 1. X 2. X 3. X 4. O 5. O 6. O 7. O 8. X

4 Learning to Summarize. Page 237.

Arrange students in groups of four to practice creating summaries. You may want to assign paragraphs to the groups. Allow 10-15 minutes for groups to read and summarize their paragraphs. Have a volunteer from each group read aloud its summary. If several groups have summarized the same paragraphs, compare and contrast the different versions. Discuss any differences.

Sample Answers:

1. The laws about the privacy of e-mail are different from the legal regulations concerning letters and phone conversations. Police cannot read e-mail messages without a warrant. But employers can keep a list of employee's secret passwords because e-mail done at work is owned by the employer. Companies can monitor employees' e-mail.

2. Electronic surveillance can be used for good and bad-to solve crimes or to watch employees at work. The surveillance systems can help find lost children or accident victims. Employers can use the systems to watch workers, but it can cause employees stress and it invades their privacy.

3. Entertainment equipment might cause airplane electronic communication problems. Important information about temperature and air speed have been lost from computers during flights. Some think that electronic games, portable computers, CD plays may be causing the problems.

4. Biotechnology creates new foods that are better in some ways but may be unsafe. Scientists combine genes to make fruits and vegetables that stay on the plant longer, taste better, not get soft quickly. Some people are afraid that these new combinations of genes and the DNA material may cause diseases later on.

Discussing the Reading

5 Small Group Discussion. Page 237.

Arrange students in groups of four to discuss the questions. Set a time limit of 15-20 minute. Circulate among the groups, giving assistance as needed. Have a volunteer from each group summarize the most interesting points discussed.

Answers will vary.

Talk It Over

Read aloud the instructions. Have students first go through and rank the different developments and inventions on their own. Then have students discuss their rankings in small groups. Encourage students to explain and give reasons to support their rankings. Go over the responses with the whole class. Were any answers the same? For which categories were the answers similar?

Part 3 Vocabulary and Language Learning Skills

1 Understanding Word Use in Context. Page 240.

After reading the instructions, go over some of the definitions, pointing out the parts of speech and definition numbers. Then have students

complete the exercise individually or in pairs. Go
over the answers with the whole class.

Answers:
2. n.1; n.2
3. v; adj. 3; adj. 2
4. n.1; v.1
5. n.2
6. n.2; v.1; v.3
7. n.1; v. 1; n.2
8. n.3; n.1
9. n.3; n.2; v.1
10 n.1; n.3; v.1

2 Understanding Word Use in Context. Page 242.

Read the instructions and have students work
individually on the exercise. Go over the answers
and have students justify their answers.

Answers: 1. a 2. d 3. b 4. f 5. e 6. c
7. i 8. k 9. g 10. j 11. h

3 Understanding Word Use in Context. Page 243.

Point out the chart and examples in the chart as
you read through the instructions together.
Students can work individually or in pairs to
complete the chart, using dictionaries as needed.
Go over the answers together.

Sample Answers:
Part of Speech: 5. adj. 6. v. 7. n. 8. v. 9.
n. 10. n. 11. n. 12. n.

Definition:
6. to call on a telephone
7. the act of delivering
8. to give a computer a program or set of instructions
9. a television show
10. an antenna that is shaped like a dish
11. a small computer for personal use
12. a machine that uses sounds

Example:
2. The convicted man spent two years in jail for his crime.
3. There is a problem with this computer terminal because I can't connect the cables to it.
4. You can send messages electronically through the computer.
5. There are some potential problems with genetically altered foods which scientists should study.
11. Most students use a microcomputer for preparing papers for class and for e-mailing their friends.

4 Real-Life Reading: Technology Instructions. Page 244.

Read together the instructions. Then ask students
to look over the instructions on page 244-245.
They should underline the verbs in the
instructions and then circle other words that are
new or difficult. Have volunteers ask about
words they circled. Invite others to suggest
examples or to explain the meanings. Arrange
students in small groups to practice explaining
how to use the VCR for the different operations.
Review the questions that can be used to ask
information about the technology instructions.
Where is the...? What do I do first? What's next?
When do I...? Which button should I press? Ask
volunteers to explain the different operations to
the class.

Answers:
Basic Playback:
1. turn on (TV); set (channel)
2. insert (video cassette)
3. press (PLAY button)
4. use (TRACKING control); adjust (picture or sound)
5. adjust (PICTURE sharpness control)

Basic Recording:
1. Turn on (TV); set (channel)
2. Push (POWER on)
3. Insert (video cassette tape)

Chapter 11

4. Set (TV/VCR to VCR)

5. Press (CHANNEL select buttons); set (Tape Speed Selector)

6. Press (REC button)

7. Set (TV/VCR button); use (channel select buttons)

Timer Recording:
1. Make sure (power); set (TV to channel)

2. Set (tape speed)

3. Set (recorder timer)

4. Push (buttons for time)

5. Turn off (TV and VCR); record (program)

5 More Real-Life Reading. Page 246.

Ask students to bring in examples of other instructions or other practical reading materials related to science and technology. Students may also want to look for examples on the Internet. Encourage students to share the samples that they found and talk about any new vocabulary that they learned from the reading materials.

Part 4 Personal Stories and Humor

1 The Trouble with Technology. Page 246.

Have students to make predictions about the content based on the title and illustrations in this exercise. Have students read the first selection. As a group, summarize the reading. Then ask questions about important details. What types of products is the writer interested in? Why do you think he is fascinated with technological equipment and devices? Why does he call these things "toys"? Are the manuals easy to read? Who usually can help him read and understand the devices? What does he do when there is a mechanical or electronic problem? What does he read after he loses interest in the new machines and devices? Do you think he has done this often?

Repeat the procedure with the other selection. Ask questions about the content or have students prepare their own questions about the reading for others in the class to answer.

Have students write their own opinions of technology and problems people have with technology. Use questions to guide them as needed. What types of technology do you use? How did you learn to use them? Do you often buy technological devices? What have you bought or what would you like to buy? How do you (can you) learn about these devices? Why do you think people find the manuals so difficult to understand? Encourage students to share their writing with others in the class.

2 The Humor of Science and Technology. Page 248.

Read the first item on page 249 and have students give their interpretations of the main joke. Discuss the other definitions with the whole class or have students work in small groups to talk about their ideas. As a class, summarize the jokes and students' reactions to them.

Answers will vary.

Video Activities: Sight for the Blind

Before You Watch

Arrange students in small groups. Read the questions aloud and ask students to talk about their opinions about the blindness and other physical challenges in their small groups. Have students report to the class their answers.

Watch [on video]

Ask them to read questions. Then play the video and have them write their answers. Review the answers together.

Answers: 1. blind men 2. It helps him see. He can see light. 3. 62, 25 4. one

Watch Again [on video]

Have students read the statements and choices. Then replay the video and have students circle the correct answers. Go over the answers.

Answers: 1. c 2. c 3. a 4. drive 5. b

After You Watch

Have students complete the matching exercise. Go over the answers with the group.

Answers: 1. e 2. f 3. b 4. c 5. d 6. a

The Global Consumer

Goals

- **Read about and discuss advertising**
- **Organize points using an outline**
- **Understand main idea**
- **Recognize exaggeration of details**
- **Identify topics and main idea**
- **Recognize author's point of view**
- **Infer meaning**
- **Summarize**
- **Understand surveys and questionnaires**
- **Express personal experiences and opinions about businesses**

Part 1 The Advertising of a Product

Before You Read

1 Discussing the Picture. Page 252.

Arrange students in small groups to answer the questions about the picture on page 252. After the groups have finished their discussions, ask a volunteer from each group report the group's responses. List vocabulary on the board. Guide students to summarize the responses. Encourage students to talk about their own experiences related to advertising and choosing products.

Sample Answers:

1. The person is in a supermarket or department store. He's trying to choose which product he should buy for washing clothes.

2. He's confused because there are so many signs for so many products made by different companies that claim to do the same thing, so he doesn't know which one is the best buy or will work the best.

3. He's looking at detergent for cleaning clothes.

4. I think these products are all very similar.

2 Thinking about the Answers. Page 252.

Read the questions aloud and call on volunteers to suggest possible answers and to make predictions about the reading. Remind students that these questions will help guide them as they read the selection and work on the exercises. Point out key vocabulary: *product, advertising, advertisers, influences*. Record students' responses and ideas on an overhead project or on a large piece of paper. Encourage students to develop their own pre-reading questions about the reading selection. You may want to review these questions and responses later after students have read the selection.

Sample Answers:

1. Some influences are advertising, words and colors on packaging, names of companies.

2. From advertising, you can learn about the product: what it's used for, some of the materials used in the product, some advantages of the product over competitors.

3. To sell products, advertisers use some misinformation, claim the product will make you better, use colors and words that are popular and that attract attention.

4. Everyone is affected by advertising.

3 Vocabulary Preview. Page 253.

As you read the words aloud, ask students to circle the ones they don't know. Ask volunteers suggest the meanings of the new words. Tell students to look for the words as they complete the reading. Later, have students come back to this list and check their understanding of their circled words.

Read

4 The Advertising of a Product. Page 253. [on tape/CD]

Play the tape or CD as students follow along in their books. Pause the tape or CD after every paragraph to ask comprehension questions and to point out key vocabulary words. Listen a second time as students read along again.

After You Read

5 Outlining Points. Page 254.

Review the purpose and organization of an outline. Read the instructions aloud. Point out the numbers I, II, III, and IV; capital letters, and 1, 2, 3, and so on in the outline. Then have students complete the rest of the exercise. Go over the answers together.

Sample Answers:

I. B. Most products are about the same in price and quality.

II. Advertising tells people about the products.

    A. Consumers learn about the benefits.

    B. Advertisers hide the disadvantages.

    C. Advertising doesn't say what is real. (It confuses our sense of reality.)

III. Advertisers use many methods to get consumers to buy the products.

    A. People are afraid that if they don't buy the product, they will not have friends or have a good life.

    B. People buy products because they want to become better and more beautiful.

    C. People buy packages with certain words and colors.

IV. Advertising affects everyone.

Main Idea: Advertisements are carefully planned to attract attention and buyers.

6 Understanding the Main Idea. Page 255.

Read the instructions aloud before having students complete the exercise. Encourage students to look back at the reading selection to check for stated and implied information. Go over the answers with the whole class.

Answers: 1. X 2. O 3. X 4. O 5. O

2. Advertisements provide us with information about the product and sometimes misinformation.

4. If you use Zoom toothpaste, there will still be problems in your life.

5. "The Psychology of Selling" might be an important course in many business colleges.

7 Recognizing Exaggeration of Details. Page 255.

Read the instructions aloud and go over the example with the students. Be they understand the meaning of exaggeration. You may want to have them suggest other examples from advertising or daily life. Then have students complete the exercise. Go over the answers.

Answers:
First Part - 1. b 2. c 3. a 4. c 5. b
Second Part - 1. a, c, d 2. a, b, c, d 3. b, c 4. c 5. b, c

Discussing the Reading

8 Small Group Discussion. Page 257.

Encourage students to talk about their own experiences with commercials and advertising. Arrange students in groups of four. Set a time limit for the small group discussions. As groups talk about their answers together, circulate among the groups, listening and giving assistance as needed. When all groups are finished, ask a volunteer from each group to summarize their ideas.

Answers will vary.

Part 2 Smart Shopping

Before You Read

1 Vocabulary Preview. Page 258.
Read the words aloud. Students can underlines words they already know and circle the ones they don't know. Tell students to look for these words in the next reading selection. Students can return back to this list and check their understanding of the circled words after completing the reading selection.

Read

2 Reviewing Topics and Main Ideas. Page 258. [on tape/CD]
Read together the instructions and the summary of main points. Remind students of the purpose of this exercise-to determine the topic of each paragraph (a title) and to state the main idea. Play the tape or CD of the reading selection as students follow along in their books. Stop the tape after every paragraph and have students choose a title for each selection. Go over the answers.

Sample Answers:
• Read Before Buying
• Generic or Brand Name?
• Read the Small Print!
• Consumers' Rights

Replay the tape and have students follow along again in their books. Ask some comprehension questions and point out key vocabulary words in

each of the paragraphs. Then have students write the main idea for each selection.

Sample Answers:
• Shoppers should read and compare information from ads, labels, and packages before buying items.

• Customers can save money by buying generic items and by doing their shopping at discount stores.

• Consumers should question advertisements to be sure they are getting all the important information.

• There are laws to protect customers from misleading and false advertisements.

After You Read

3 Viewpoint. Page 260.
Read the instructions and discuss the meaning of "point of view." If needed, ask students if the author of the selection thinks advertising is good or bad. Have volunteers locate passages from the reading to support their ideas. Then have students complete the exercise. Go over students' responses.

Sample Answer: It is not a reliable source of information on products, and consumers need to be aware of how advertising may mislead people.

4 Inferring the Meaning. Page 260.
Before students complete the exercise, read together the instructions. As you go over the answers, encourage students to point out parts of the reading selection that support their answers.

Answers:
1. X 2. O 3. X 4. X 5. O 6. X 7. X 8. X 9. X 10. X

5 Learning to Summarize. Page 261.
Read the instructions together. Encourage students to use their main-idea statements from Exercise 2 (pages 259-260) as a starting point for their summarizing. Arrange students in groups of

four to practice summarizing. You may want to assign paragraphs to the groups. Allow 10-15 minutes for groups to read and summarize their paragraphs. Then, ask a volunteer from each group to read aloud its summary. If several groups have summarized the same paragraphs, compare and contrast the different versions. Discuss any differences.

Sample Answers:

- Shoppers should read and compare ads, labels, and packages before buying items. In ads, shoppers can find about which items are on sale. Shoppers should also read the labels and packages to learn about the ingredients. They should also compare the prices of different size containers and different brands. They will be able to save money by doing these things.

- Customers can save money by buying generic items and shopping at discount stores. Generic products are less expensive because the manufacturer spends less money on the containers and advertising. Brand name items are more expensive. Discount stores may not be as fancy as other stores, but the prices are often lower.

- Consumers should question advertisements to be sure they are getting all the information. They should read all the small print. They should check if the ad has real information or is just a pretty picture. After consumers know these things, they can make a good choice.

- There are laws to protect consumers from misleading and false advertisement. A store must have a reasonable number of items that are on sale. Items in the store should be like the pictures on ads. Ads need to state if there are limits on how many you can buy or to state if the items are used or defective. The laws help consumers get what they pay for.

Discussing the Reading

6 Small Group Discussion. Page 261.

Allow 15-20 minutes for students to work in groups of four to discuss their answers to the questions. Circulate among the groups, giving assistance as needed. Ask a volunteer from each group to summarize the most interesting points discussed.

Answers will vary.

Talk It Over

Read aloud the instructions. Have students suggest samples of favorite advertising slogans they have heard and seen. Then students can work in pairs to match the slogans with the products. Remind them to look for clues in the slogans for how the product is used. As you go over the answers, have students explain their reasons for their responses

Answers: 1. j 2. e 3. c 4. i 5. a 6. b 7. d 8. g 9. f 10. h 11. l 12. k

Part 3 Vocabulary and Language Learning Skills

1 Reviewing Vocabulary-Learning Methods. Page 262.

Read together the instructions and the summary of main points about vocabulary learning. Have students complete the exercise. Go over the answers with the whole class.

Answers:

2. in-; verb; It follows a noun and says what the noun does.; tells; information (n.), informer (n.), informative (adj.); The teacher informs us when we are going to have a test.

3. con-; -ers; noun; It is the object of the verb.; consume or use things; consume

(v.), consumption (n.); Many consumers check labels before being items.

4. pro-; noun; It is the object of the verb.; things; produce; producer (n.), production (n.), productive (adj.), productivity (n.), productively (adv.); We saw many new products in the store last weekend.

5. -able; adjective; It describes the products.; in good supply; obtainable; unavailable; This computer is available for you to use.

6. available for buying; for sale; There are lots of used cars on the market right now.

7. verb; It tells what the advertising does.; to influence; keeps us from buying; This label leads me to think that the product is very good.

8. don't have enough money; I only have two dollars, so I can't afford to go out to eat tonight.

After reading the instructions, go over the examples in the chart. Students can use a dictionary as needed to complete the chart. Go over the answers together.

Answers:

2. What brand of shampoo do you use on your hair?

3. I sometimes wash my dirty laundry at home, but sometimes I take it to a laundromat.

4. v.; I have to admit that this ice cream tastes very good.; admission (n.), admittance (n.), admissible (adj.), admittedly (adv.)

5. n.; His sense of hearing was not good because he was wearing headphones.; senseless (adj.), sensible (adj.), sensitive (adj.), sensor (n.), sensory (adj.), sensibly (adv.) sensibility (n.)

6. adj.; nice looking; ugly; attract (v.), attraction (n.) attractively (adv.), attractiveness (n.)

7. adj.; dumb, not smart; intelligent; stupidity (n.), stupidly (adv.) stupor (n.)

8. v.; to participate in a game or contest; competition (n.), competitive (adj.), competitively (adv.), competitor (n.), competence (n.), competency (n.), competent (adj.), competently (adv.)

9. adv.; in a hostile manner; passively or calmly; aggressive (adj.), aggression (n.), aggressiveness (n.), aggressor (n.), aggressiveness (n.).

10. v.; to enlarge or make something more important; My brother exaggerates when he tells about the size of the fish he catches.

2 Real-Life Reading: Surveys and Questionnaires. Page 266.

If possible, bring in of surveys and questionnaires. Have students talk about any experiences they have had filling out these items. Talk about who gives surveys and why they ask people to fill them out. Read together the instructions. Tell students to underline words they know and circle words that they don't know on the questionnaire. Then arrange students in small groups to discuss the meanings of new words and to take the questionnaire. Have the group decide who is probably giving the questionnaire and how the information might be useful to them. Ask volunteers to summarize their groups' discussions.

3 More Real-Life Reading. Page 266.

Encourage students to look for and bring in examples of other real-life reading materials related to shopping, advertising, and questionnaires. Students can share their samples with the class and talk about any new vocabulary that they learned.

Part 4 Personal Stories and Humor

1 Big Business. Page 267.

Have students to make predictions about the content based on the title and illustrations in the exercise. Have students read the first selection. Then ask comprehension questions. *Who went to "market day"? Why was it a good place to shop? How was it like a festival? What types of advertising were at the market? Why was it like a theater? Do you go to markets? Where and when? What types of things can you buy there?* As a group, summarize the reading.

Repeat the procedure with the other selection. Ask questions about the content or have students prepare their own questions about the readings for others in the class to answer.

Have students write their own experiences and opinions about advertising, shopping, and markets. Use questions to guide them as needed. Encourage students to share their writing with others in the class.

2 The Humor of Advertising. Page 270.

Read the instructions together. Point out that the signs start at the bottom of each picture and go up as if you are driving past them on the road. Then ask students to look at the first set of signs. Have a volunteer read them aloud. Have students give their interpretations of the joke. Explain phrases as needed: *of late, dates.* What is the advertiser implying about using Burma-Shave?

Ask the questions and go over the answers. Then arrange students in groups of four to read and discuss the other sets of signs. Have volunteers share their groups' responses with the whole class.

Sample Answers:
Ad A.
1. Dedicate, late

2. The signs are for me who haven't gone out with girls lately.
3.—5. Answers will vary.

Ad B.
1. adore, sore
2. A girl will not get mad if a boy with a beard or whiskers kisses, but her face will be sore (from the scratchy whiskers).

Ad C.
1. blind, behind
2. The person in the car behind is following very closely, does he just want to be friends or does he have problems seeing?

Ad D.
1. pink, drink
2. People who drink and drive may end up dead with pretty flowers on their graves.

Ad E.
1. Down, town
2. When you buy Burma-Shave, you've bought the best product in town.

Ad F.
1. Clerks, works
2. The person heard about Burma-Shave from store clerks, so he tried it, and found out that it really does work.

Ad G.
1. Kiddo, widow
2. People pay money for insurance, but if you drive carelessly and die, you don't get the insurance money, but your wife (widow) will get it.

Ad H.
1. Bounce, announce
2. They are announcing a new product that will wake you up in the morning. It's Burma-Shave lotion.

Video Activities: Spoiled Kids

Before You Watch

Arrange students in small groups. Read the questions aloud and ask students to talk about their thoughts about parent-child relationships in their small groups. Have students report to the class their answers.

Answers will vary.

Watch [on video]

Ask them to read the questions. Remind them to think about the questions as they view the video. Allow students to discuss their answers to the questions in small groups. Then, review the answers together with the whole class.

Answers:
1. Bret has Nintendo and video games. Jessica has a phone, a radio, a tape player
2. from their parents and with their own money
3. psychologist
4. They have the money; they love their children; they feel guilty; they have trouble saying no.

Watch Again [on video]

Have students read the statements. Then replay the video and have students match the statements to the people who said them. Go over the answers.

Answers: 1. c 2. d 3. a 4. a 5. b 6. a

After You Watch

Read together the instructions, reminding students that *affluenza* is not a real word. Then have students work in pairs to prepare their own definition of it based on the words *affluence* and *influenza*. Go over the answers with the group.

Answers:

Affluence: a large supply or money and things

Influenza: a contagious disease with fever and inflamed lungs; the flu

Affluenza: a disease of having too much money and things

Reading Placement Test

Part 1 Determining Meaning and Usage from Context

Circle the letter of the best word or words to complete each sentence.

Example:

Public schools are forbidden to teach _____ , whereas parochial schools are required to do so.

    a. religious

    b. spiritual

    c. mathematics

    (d.) religion

1. The puppy was very _____ with the children.

    a. calmness

    b. calm

    c. calamity

    d. calms

2. The father harshly _____ every boy who went out with his daughter.

    a. judge

    b. judging

    c. to judge

    d. judged

3. The patient was extremely _____ and had to be subdued.

    a. agitated

    b. agitates

    c. agitating

    d. agitate

4. **Children who wish to _____ or achieve greatness must have drive and work hard.**

   a. drive a car

   b. fail

   c. excel

   d. go home

5. **Poodles, German Shepherds, Golden Retrievers are different types of _____.**

   a. canines

   b. felines

   c. dogs

   d. a and c

6. **If you are having trouble logging onto the Internet you might want to check out your _____.**

   a. modem configuration string

   b. video monitor

   c. word processing program

   d. none of the above

7. **Spending time reading newspapers and _____ is a good way to keep up with current events.**

   a. historical novels

   b. ancient texts

   c. classic books

   d. other periodicals

8. **The enlightened ministers, Catholic priests, Jewish rabbis, and Buddhist monks _____.**

   a. belong to an ecumenical organization

   b. belong to the same denomination

   c. had identical religious training

   d. none of the above is possible

9. **She was a very _____ young child who could read university texts by the time that she was nine years old.**

   a. precocious

   b. illiterate

   c. developmentally delayed

   d. inadequate

10. **The mechanic was confident and felt that it was very _____ or plausible to get the truck repaired in a week.**

    a. unpredictable

    b. unrealistic

    c. feasible

    d. surreal

Part 2 Idiomatic Expressions

Circle the letter of the best meaning of the underlined idiomatic expression.

Example:

She wanted to leave under good terms and not to <u>burn her bridges</u>.

    a. make it impossible to return because of bad feelings

    b. destroy the bridges where she had traveled previously

    c. dynamite a bridge

    d. create bridges and avenues to the future

1. **The mother told her son to be conservative and mindful of what he had since <u>a bird in the hand is worth two in the bush</u>.**

    a. Birds fly away even when you have them in your hand.

    b. Birds are worth watching and loving: the more the merrier.

    c. It is better to hold onto something you own than to leave it unattended, and rush off to try to get something unknown.

    d. Always be conservative and never go after something new.

2. **Carl's boss was against all of Carl's plans for improvement and <u>tied his hands</u>, which prevented him from doing anything innovative.**

    a. was very proactive and supportive of Carl

    b. stopped him from working well

    c. put Carl into a psychiatric hospital where straitjackets were used

    d. Carl put his boss in a straitjacket

3. **Cynthia's father adored her and considered her to be the <u>apple of his eye</u>.**

    a. felt that his daughter could find lots of apples in the trees because she had such good eyes

    b. did everything he could think of to find apples for his daughter

    c. believed that his daughter needed to eat apples to improve her eyes

    d. believed his daughter was wonderful

4. **George was mediocre at many different things; he was a <u>jack of all trades and master of none</u>.**

   a. able to do many things that women could never do

   b. a master of many trades and did many things very well

   c. could do many different things, but none especially well

   d. a master of many things and did everything except one exceptionally well

5. **She wanted to be promoted, but her hopes were <u>dashed</u> when her employer declared bankruptcy.**

   a. dreams were fulfilled

   b. depression was deferred

   c. specific wishes were no longer possible

   d. life became joyful

Part 3 Scanning for Members of Word Families

Circle the letter of the best word to complete each sentence:

Example:

_____ is a noun meaning "a place that sells baked goods."

   a. Baker

   (b.) Bakery

   c. Baked

   d. Bakes

1. _____ is a verb meaning "to become more economical."

   a. Economize

   b. Economical

   c. Economics

   d. Economically

2. _____ is a noun meaning that "someone or something has grown fully or fully developed."

   a. Mature

   b. Maturity

   c. Maturing

   d. Matured

3. _____ is a verb meaning "to take an idea or concept and apply it in other situations."

    a. Extrapolation

    b. Extricate

    c. Extrication

    d. Extrapolate

4. _____ is a noun meaning "a person who tells jokes or funny stories."

    a. Comics

    b. Comedy

    c. Comedian

    d. Comical

5. _____ is a an adjective referring to "the cells of an unborn baby."

    a. Embryo

    b. Embryonic

    c. Embryos

    d. Amoeba

Part 4 Reading Comprehension

Reading 1

Have you ever thought about where you should sit on an airplane? It is important to book your seat early so that you can select a seat that best serves your needs. Individuals traveling in first class and business class usually need to think about whether they want an aisle seat or to sit next to a window or next to the bulkhead, or wall.

If you are stuck in the economy section of the aircraft you must still consider whether you want a window, aisle, or a seat next the bulkhead. You must also take into account many different factors. You should decide whether or not you want to be in the front or rear section of the aircraft. The advantage of being near the front of the plane is that you will be able to board and deplane quickly. However, if you want to get an empty seat next to you, you should get a seat towards the rear, since people are assigned seats from the front to the rear. Please don't be discouraged if you end up with a center or middle seat since most airlines have middle seats that are a little bit wider than the window or aisle seats.

Based on the article, indicate whether each statement is true or false.

Example:
_F_ **This short article was written by someone who is unfamiliar with air travel.**

1. ___ A bulkhead is not considered to be a wall.

2. ___ This article is about seat selection in both the economy and business or first class sections of an airplane.

3. ___ According to the article, if you are sitting in the economy section of a plane, you always want to sit towards the front of the section.

4. ___ Seats are assigned from the rear of the aircraft forward.

5. ___ You should be very upset if you get a middle seat.

Reading 2

Have you ever wanted to do something tremendous and earth shattering? You might think that you need to discover a cure for cancer, construct a huge monument, or be the first to fly around the world in a hot air balloon for your activity to count as being remarkable. Actually there are many very simple acts of kindness that can completely save a person's heart or life. My sister was recently touring Germany when she received some very devastating news. It was probably the worst news of her life. She was completely alone, in a strange land with no friends or family. A stranger, a big-sister-type figure, took her in and offered her both an ear and a cup of Earl Grey tea. That simple act gave my sister some of the courage that she needed to tackle her troubles. So the next time you want to do something great, simply take time to be kind to your fellow man or woman.

Based on the article, indicate whether each statement is true or false.

Example:
_F_ **We know for a fact that the author had a sister and a brother.**

1. ___ If something is earth shattering, it is unimportant.

2. ___ A cure for cancer is noteworthy.

3. ___ Simple acts are never great acts.

4. ___ The author's sister was given some very bad news while she was traveling.

5. ___ The stranger didn't offer the author's sister Earl Grey tea.

Reading 3

The Visually Impaired

Individuals who are blind, or those who are low vision, as well as those with less severe visual impairments, have benefited from a variety of key developments that have occurred in Europe and the United States during the past couple of centuries. Low vision refers to individuals who have very limited sight and it does not have anything to do with whether items are high or low to the ground. The effort to assist the visually challenged began in the latter 1700s, when a gentleman by the name of Victor Hauly committed himself to teach the blind. This noble act occurred after he witnessed people being paraded around as court jesters or struggling on the streets as beggars. Mr. Hauly founded a residential school for blind children that featured teaching children how to read with raised print. Following the precedent set by Mr. Hauly, Mr. Samuel Gridley Howe founded the world-renowned Perkins School for the Blind in 1821 in the United States. A variety of curricula and methods were both piloted and refined at the Perkins School. Anne Sullivan and her well-known pupil, Helen Keller, spent several years at the Perkins School.

A little over a dozen years after the establishment of the Perkins School, a French man named Louis Braille created the Braille's system. The Braille system, as it is now referred to, is probably the most successful method for teaching touch-reading and has survived the test of time. It is simple, utilizing a six-dot cell system, but should never be perceived as simplistic.

In the second half of the nineteenth century, one of the major advances for the visually impaired was not targeted at blind or very low vision children but rather at children who appeared on the surface to have "normal" vision. In the 1860s, a Dutch ophthalmologist invented or developed the Snellen chart. This was an important creation since it was and currently still is the most widely used device for visual acuity screening of school age children.

The first major development for the severely visually impaired took place between 1900 and 1913. Classes in public schools were opened in Boston, Chicago, and Cleveland for children who were blind or had low vision. This was a significant development since several local school systems began to recognize that the government had an obligation to provide education for children with severe visual impairments. Following the establishment of the public school classes east of the Mississippi River, other school systems followed suit.

The next trend to provide blind individuals with government supported services occurred in 1932 when the U.S. Library of Congress made talking books available to all legally blind individuals. Also in the 1930s, a California school district employed itinerant teachers to help students with visual impairments function in regular education classrooms. During this time period, also in the U.S., there was the inauguration of orientation and mobility services including a white cane to help people function in the community.

In the second half of the 20th century, the Perkins braillewriter was invented at the Perkins School for the Blind. The braillewriter made it possible for individuals sitting at simple machines to transcribe books into a touch-reading format. This increased literacy among those with severe visual impairments. It is hoped that the advances for the visually impaired continue well into the 21st century.

Circle the letter of the best word or words to complete each sentence.

Example:
The best title for this article could possibly be:

a. Key Developments Impacting Those Without Visual Impairments
b. Key Developments Benefiting Those with Visual Impairments
c. The Visually Challenged in Your Community
d. People Who Help the Visually Impaired

1. **Individuals with low vision _____.**

   a. can only see things that are low to the ground

   b. have very minimal sight and can only see things that are low to the ground

   c. have very minimal sight

   d. none of the above

2. **From the article, one can assume that Cleveland is _____.**

   a. within 100 miles of Boston

   b. within 100 miles of Chicago

   c. east of the Mississippi

   d. all of the above

3. **There have been certain residential schools founded for the blind. These include _____.**

   a. the school founded by Mr. Hauly

   b. the school founded by Mr. Perkins

   c. the schools founded by Mr. Gridley Howe and Mr. Perkins

   d. the schools founded Mr. Hauly and Mr. Gridley Howe

4. **All of the advances mentioned in this article took place in _____.**

   a. Europe

   b. the United States

   c. the United States and Europe

   d. none of the above

5. **The Braille system is _____.**

   a. simplistic

   b. simple

   c. simple and simplistic

   d. neither simple nor simplistic

6. **The Snellen chart is an important development _____.**

   a. because it helped children who were completely blind and had no vision

   b. because it only helped low vision children

   c. because it helped to identify children who both have visual impairments and attend regular public schools

   d. because an ophthalmologist was involved in the creation

7. **Although specific information was not given, one could assume that _____.**

   a. Dr. Snellen did not invent the Snellen chart

   b. Mr. Perkins developed the Snellen chart

   c. Dr. Snellen invented the Snellen chart

   d. Mr. Perkins and Mr. Braille developed the Snellen chart

8. **Talking books are only available for those _____.**

   a. who are legally blind

   b. who can not be legally blind

   c. who have hearing aids and are legally blind

   d. who have any visual impairments, even minor ones

9. **The white cane _____.**

   a. was designed to help the severely visually impaired students stay out of the community

   b. was designed to keep the blind in residential schools

   c. was inaugurated by the president of the Perkins school

   d. was designed to help individuals with visual impairments function in the community

10. **The Perkins braillewriter _____.**

   a. was the only invention in the 20th century that gave blind individuals access to books

   b. was invented by Mr. Perkins

   c. helped blind individuals have access to the printed word

   d. none of the above

Reading 4

The Critic's Corner

This week, I will be writing about a topic near and dear to my heart as well as the heart of my children. Don't underestimate the power or value of children's literature or "kiddie lit" as it is sometimes referred. Many individuals find it surprising that children's literature, even books with little text, frequently encompass social themes that span from environmental studies to psychology or sociology. For example, "The Giving Tree" by Shel Silverstein is a very simple but elegant black and white picture book that tells the story of a boy and a tree that are mutually dependent upon one another. As the story unfolds, the man exploits the tree, while the tree remains gracious and benevolent towards the man. This book makes a powerful statement concerning man's disregard and downright callousness towards the environment.

Judith Viorst, a satirist, has written a charming picture book entitled "Alexander and the Terrible, Horrible, No Good, Very Bad Day." Her work, illustrated with black and white drawings, deals with the frustrations confronting a very young boy. Through the voice of a child, she reveals the emotional issues impacting children including sibling rivalry, parental approval, and unrealistic teacher expectations. This book is invaluable for those wishing to study the psychological makeup of young children, mainly boys but also girls.

Another book with a minimal amount of print worth checking out is "A Chair for My Mother" by Vera Williams. The story of a family who has lost all of their belongings in a fire is told, in part, through brightly colored illustrations accompanied by text. The community pulls together to get the family back on their feet. In addition, the family helps itself reach a goal through hard work and stick-to-itiveness. This book addresses some key sociological support systems, including the extended family and the community.

So the next time you are in a bookstore or library, take a deep breath and a moment to stop and browse the children's book section.

Based on the article, circle the letter of the best answer to each question.

Example:
What is the main topic of this article?
a. Children's Literature
b. Remedies for Social Problems
c. Environmental Studies
d. none of the above

1. How does the writer of the article feel about children's literature?
a. The writer believes that it is a frivolous genre that should be dismissed.
b. The writer believes that it has a great deal of merit.
c. It isn't clear.
d. The writer feels that it should be rejected from people's hearts.

2. In the first paragraph the words *mutually dependent* are used. In this context, what does *mutually dependent* mean?
a. Both sides do NOT need one another.
b. One side needs the other.
c. Both sides need one another.
d. Everyone is dependent upon the environment.

3. Which book deals with issues impacting the environment?
a. "The Giving Tree"
b. "A Chair for My Mother"
c. both a and b
d. none of the above

4. Which books are illustrated with black and white drawings?
a. "The Giving Tree"
b. "Alexander and the Terrible, Horrible, No Good, Very Bad Day"
c. "A Chair for my Mother"
d. a and b

5. According to the article, what can one assume?

    a. The writer has some familiarity with children's literature.

    b. The writer has no familiarity with children's literature.

    c. The writer doesn't want to read any more children's books.

    d. The writer checks out a lot of books from the library.

6. What did Judith Viorst, a mother herself, write?

    a. a book using a mother's voice

    b. a book only suitable for mothers to read

    c. a book using the "voice" of a child

    d. a book that could never have been written by a satirist

7. What was the psychological pressure, or pressures, mentioned in Judith Viorst's book?

    a. sibling rivalry

    b. parental approval

    c. teacher satisfaction

    d. a and b but not c

8. What happened to the family in Vera Williams's book?

    a. They suffered from a fire.

    b. They survived the fire.

    c. a and b

    d. none of the above

9. What does Vera Williams use to tell her story?

    a. only text to write her story

    b. only text to relay her message

    c. only illustrations to relay her message

    c. text and illustrations to convey her message

10. What is meant by the term *stick-to-itiveness*?

    a. lazy

    b. someone involved in sticky situations

    c. someone who cannot work hard

    d. someone who keeps on working until a goal is achieved

Name _____   Date _____

1. Match each word with its meaning. (5 points)

___ 1. institution of higher education   a. grants

___ 2. international   b. countries

___ 3. scholarships   c. professors

___ 4. quizzes   d. university

___ 5. instructors   e. in a foreign place

___ 6. facilities   f. points

___ 7. informal   g. foreign

___ 8. abroad   h. tests

___ 9. nations   i. casual

___ 10. scores   j. buildings

2. Write T for true statements and F for false statements. (5 points)

___ 1. Most colleges and universities don't want international students.

___ 2. International students only go to colleges and universities in the United States.

___ 3. International students bring different customs, ideas, and opinions to the schools.

___ 4. Most colleges and universities have resource centers, libraries, and other facilities for their students.

___ 5. All instructors dress casually and teach in a relaxed atmosphere.

3. Circle the letter of the correct word. (5 points)

1. Tuition _____ the fee or charge for instruction.

   a. are   b. is   c. pay

2. International students _____ hard.

   a. study   b. studies   c. is

3. Where _____ the Physical Education offices?

   a. are   b. is   c. find

4. Students with the highest scores on tests _____ the best universities.

   a. are   b. attend   c. attends

5. There _____ many international students in the United States.

   a. are   b. is   c. be

4. Write the facility or service you would use. Use the choices from the box. (5 points)

Admissions and Records	Career Planning	Computer Center
Bookstore	Financial Aid Office	Gymnasium

1. Where can I go to exercise or play basketball? _____

2. Where should I go to register for classes? _____

3. Where should I go to use the Internet? _____

4. Where should I go to buy some textbooks? _____

5. Where should I go to ask about loans and grants? _____

5. Write answers to the questions. Use complete sentences. (5 points)

1. What kind of school do you attend?

   _____

   _____

2. Where do you live?

   _____

   _____

3. Do you prefer a hard program of studies or an informal program?

   _____

   _____

4. Which school facility do you think is the most important?

   _____

   _____

5. Why do international students go to school abroad?

   _____

   _____

Name _____   **Date** _____

1. Match each word with its meaning. (5 points)

___	1. an effect	a.	sicknesses
___	2. to influence	b.	damp, wet
___	3. to increase	c.	to have an effect on something; to change
___	4. researcher	d.	full of power and strength
___	5. diseases	e.	a result
___	6. forceful	f.	a person who studies a subject or problem
___	7. depressing	g.	the weather
___	8. humid	h.	feeling sad or not feeling happy
___	9. moody	i.	to become greater in number or power
___	10. atmospheric conditions	j.	the condition of feeling sad or sorrowful

2. Write *T* for true statements and *F* for false statements. (5 points)

___ 1. Weather conditions do not influence people's health, thinking, or feelings.

___ 2. Strong winds in Russia increase the number of strokes and heart attacks.

___ 3. Colds and flu are diseases that increase during warm weather.

___ 4. In northern regions, people feel less tired in the winter.

___ 5. Seasonal Affective Disorder may be caused by too little sun and light during the daytime.

3. Circle the letter of the correct word. (5 points)

1. The earth's climate _____ slowly.
   a. are changing   b. is changing   c. change

2. Global warming and El Niño _____ an effect on the earth and weather.
   a. has   b. is having   c. are having

3. The temperature of the earth _____ up.
   a. going   b. is going   c. are going

4. Cars and factories _____ more carbon dioxide into the air.
   a. are putting   b. is putting   c. putting

5. We _____ some of the problems.

    a. are causing   b. is causing   c. causing

4. Write the category for the items. Use the choices from the box. (5 points)

continents	oceans	weather
storms	climate	islands

1. hurricanes, cyclones, blizzards _____

2. Atlantic, Pacific, Indians _____

3. rain, sun, fog, clouds _____

4. Asia, South America, Europe _____

5. temperate, tropical, polar _____

5. Write answers to the questions. Use complete sentences. (5 points)

1. What kind of weather do you like best? Why?

_____

_____

2. What is the climate like in your area of the world?

_____

_____

3. Does weather affect the way you feel? If so, how?

_____

_____

4. What are some illnesses or diseases that are caused by certain weather conditions?

_____

_____

5. What types of severe weather and storm have you seen or experienced?

_____

_____

Name _____   **Date** _____

1. Match each word with its meaning. (5 points)

___	1. nutrition	a.	easy to reach or use
___	2. habits	b.	to bring forth; to cause to exist
___	3. ingredients	c.	usual practices or behavior
___	4. dairy	d.	to consist of or include
___	5. contain	e.	diet; the study of food and nourishment
___	6. produce	f.	causing growth and development
___	7. convenient	g.	items used in a mixture
___	8. healthful	h.	eating places with the same name
___	9. nourishing		and company owner
___	10. fast-food chains	i.	relating to milk and milk products
		j.	contributing to good health

2. Write *T* for true statements and *F* for false statements. (5 points)

___ 1. A person's diet is his or her usual food choices.

___ 2. All people like fast food because it is inexpensive and convenient.

___ 3. Fast food is always healthful.

___ 4. Foods with high nutritional value have a lot of fiber, vitamins, and minerals.

___ 5. The global diet is becoming less healthful.

3. Circle the letter of the correct word. (5 points)

1. Food should _____ fresh and natural.

   a. is   b. be   c. being

2. Families are _____ more meals at home.

   a. prepare   b. prepares   c. preparing

3. Many people like to _____ on candy and cookies.

   a. snack   b. snacking   c. snacks

4. Food companies are _____ more nutritious food.

   a. produce   b. produces   c. producing

5. Too much fat and sugar can _____ health problems.

   a. increase   b. increases   c. increasing

4. **Write the category for the items. Use the choices from the box. (5 points)**

junk foods	natural foods	nutrients
convenience foods	high fat foods	high protein foods

1. _____ : meat, chicken, fish

2. _____ : water, protein, carbohydrates, vitamins, minerals

3. _____ : candy, cookies, potato chips

4. _____ : canned, frozen, or packaged foods

5. _____ : items without chemical substances

5. **Write answers to the questions. Use complete sentences. (5 points)**

1. What types of food do you like?

   _____

   _____

2. Where do you usually eat?

   _____

   _____

3. Do you often eat fast food or convenience foods? Why or why not?

   _____

   _____

4. What foods do you think are the most nutritious?

   _____

   _____

5. Are there certain types of food that you don't eat? What are they?

   _____

   _____

Name _____   **Date** _____

1. Match each word with its meaning. (5 points)

___	1. advantages	a. not often; rarely
___	2. tourists	b. to give a direction or signal
___	3. the countryside	c. rude; discourteous
___	4. to motion	d. people who travel for pleasure
___	5. gestures	e. without turns or curves
___	6. impolite	f. things that are helpful or useful
___	7. confused	g. a feeling or understanding of how to find places
___	8. seldom	
___	9. straight	h. a rural region without large cities
___	10. sense of direction	i. movements of the arms, hands, or head
		j. mixed-up; disordered

2. Write *T* for true statements and *F* for false statements. (5 points)

___ 1. People around the world give directions the same way.

___ 2. Tourists in Japan get confused because there are no street names.

___ 3. In the American Midwest, people give directions in distances.

___ 4. In Los Angeles, California, people measure distances in miles, kilometers, and blocks.

___ 5. Everywhere people use body language to give directions.

3. Circle the letter of the correct word. (5 points)

1. I prefer to ask _____ directions.

   a. to   b. for   c. in

2. You should turn left _____ the big hotel.

   a. at   b. on   c. in

3. The post office is _____ the bus stop.

   a. across from   b. for   c. from

4. Go another mile _____ a northeast direction.

   a. at   b. for   c. in

5. Some people will lead you _____ the post office.

   a. of   b. to   c. at

4. Write the name of the community service you would use. Use the choices from the box. (5 points)

Legal Services	Community College	Department of Motor Vehicles
Libraries	Housing	Immigrant and Refugee Services

1. Where can I register my car or get a driver's license? _____

2. Where can I borrow books? _____

3. Where can I get help with laws and the court system? _____

4. Where can I sign up for classes? _____

5. Where can I get help apartment problems? _____

5. Write answers to the questions. Use complete sentences. (5 points)

1. Do you like traveling to new places? Why or why not?

   _____

   _____

2. What do you do when you are lost in a new place?

   _____

   _____

3. Do you give directions to people? How?

   _____

   _____

4. What is a good law or rule that you know? Why do you think it is good?

   _____

   _____

5. What is a law or rule that people don't follow? Why don't they follow it?

   _____

   _____

Name _____   Date _____

1. Match each word with its meaning. (5 points)

___	1. relatives	a.	to decrease in value
___	2. couples	b.	customary way of doing things
___	3. divorces	c.	to provide money and other necessary things
___	4. widow		for care of others
___	5. decline	d.	to take into a family through a legal process
___	6. adopt	e.	people related through marriage or family
___	7. traditional	f.	the legal ending of a marriage
___	8. nuclear family	g.	a family group that includes cousins, aunts,
___	9. extended family		uncles, grandparents, and so on.
___	10. support	h.	two people who are married or very close
		i.	a family group of just parents and children
		j.	a woman whose husband has died

2. Write *T* for true statements and *F* for false statements. (5 points)

___ 1. There are only two types of families: extended families and nuclear families.

___ 2. Many women had to go to work outside of the home during World War II.

___ 3. After World War II, families become more traditional with the father working and the mother staying at home.

___ 4. The divorce rate declined and the birthrate increased since the 1960s.

___ 5. The family structure will probably change more in the future.

3. Circle the letter of the correct word. (5 points)

1. _____ 100 years ago, family structure was more traditional.

    a. For   b. In   c. Over

2. Life was difficult for families _____ the 1930s.

    a. in   b. between   c. to

3. _____ 1939 to 1945, many families were separated because of the war.

    a. After   b. Over   c. From

4. _____ World War II, family structure changed again.

    a. From   b. During   c. To

5. There have been more changes in families in the United States _____ 1960.

    a. over   b. since   c. at

4. Circle the correct word (noun or related adjective) to complete the sentence. (5 points)

1. In many cultures, there are many traditions and customs for (marriage / married).

2. It is (custom / customary) for the father to support the family in a traditional family.

3. The family group is a (universe / universal) structure in society.

4. Today, single parent families are more (community / common).

5. With the (modernization / modern) of society, families have changed.

5. Write answers to the questions. Use complete sentences. (5 points)

1. What was your family like when you were growing up?

_____

_____

2. What are some different types of family groups?

_____

_____

3. What are some reasons why family structure has changed in the past?

_____

_____

4. Is life easy or difficult for families today? Why?

_____

_____

5. What do you think is the "perfect family"?

_____

_____

Name _____   **Date** _____

1. Match each word with its meaning. (5 points)

___ 1. achievement
___ 2. weapon
___ 3. invent
___ 4. agree
___ 5. polite
___ 6. rude
___ 7. significant
___ 8. pleasantly
___ 9. proud
___ 10. magnificent

a. something used to fight
b. to have the same opinion
c. without good manners
d. nicely; agreeably
e. excellent; grand
f. feeling happy about something you own or have done or are part of
g. meaningful; important
h. with good manners
i. to create something new
j. something that is difficult to do

2. Write *T* for true statements and *F* for false statements. (5 points)

___ 1. The fine arts include architecture, music, literature, paintings, and sculpture.

___ 2. Some early important inventions were in media—TV, CDs, and the Internet.

___ 3. All important scientific and technological discoveries were in the Americas.

___ 4. Some points of culture are universal, such as food and media.

___ 5. Because of cultural diversity, people around the world celebrate the same things.

3. Circle the letter of the correct word. (5 points)

1. There are _____ people in all societies.
    a. create   b. creation   c. creative

2. Can you _____ an important invention from the past?
    a. descriptive   b. description   c. describe

3. The conversation may _____ into an argument.
    a. develop   b. development   c. developing

4. The people in the group were not in _____ about the definition of culture.
    a. agree   b. agreement   c. agreeable

5. Each person mentioned an important _____ from his or her cultural group.

   a. achieve　　　　　　b. achievable　　　　　　c. achievement

4. Write the category you would use to find these types of cultural announcements. Use the choices from the box. (5 points)

Cultural Festivals	Lectures	Music
Literary Readings	Travel Packages	Art and Architecture

1. Where should I look for information about a discussion of culture? _____

2. Where should I look for information about a poet reading some of his or her favorite poems?
   _____

3. Where should I look for information about bands and singers performing in the area?
   _____

4. Where should I look for information about exhibits of paintings and sculpture?
   _____

5. Where should I look for information about exhibits and demonstrations of traditional dances and music? _____

5. Write answers to the questions. Use complete sentences. (5 points)

1. What do you think are important elements of cultures?
   _____
   _____

2. What do you think are important contributions from ancient cultures?
   _____
   _____

3. In what ways are cultures different from each other?
   _____
   _____

4. In what ways are cultures similar to each other?
   _____
   _____

5. Why is it sometimes difficult for people of different cultures to understand each other?
   _____
   _____

Name _____   **Date** _____

1. Match each word with its meaning. (5 points)

____ 1. stress   a. all the surroundings-water, soil, air

____ 2. preservations   b. to bring back to health

____ 3. theories   c. the people that live in a place

____ 4. consume   d. something added to food to protect it

____ 5. prevent   from spoiling

____ 6. cure   e. average; not extreme

____ 7. moderate   f. to eat or drink

____ 8. environment   g. a force that strains somebody or something

____ 9. inhabitants   h. legal; logical

____ 10. valid   i. guesses based on some information

                                     j. to keep something from happening

2. Write *T* for true statements and *F* for false statements. (5 points)

____ 1. Some people in high mountainous regions live to a very old age.

____ 2. These people live in polluted environments near large cities.

____ 3. They do not work very hard outside.

____ 4. Their diets include natural foods and vegetables.

____ 5. They have a lot of worries and stress.

3. Circle the letter of the correct word. (5 points)

1. Some scientists believe the claim, _____ others think the claims are false.

    a. and   b. but   c. therefore

2. These people often work hard outside. _____ they live in a clean environment.

    a. In addition   b. In contrast   c. As a result

3. They have large extended families. _____ the groups take care of their members.

    a. Too   b. Instead   c. Therefore

4. The food is all natural, _____ they use traditional medicines and herbs.

    a. furthermore   b. even so   c. thus

5. They are farmers. _____ they work hard and are active.

    a. Similarly   b. Nevertheless   c. As a result

4. Emergency Instructions: Number the following statements in the proper order. (5 points)

_____ Make sure the person is breathing.

_____ If the person is vomiting, roll him or her onto the left side.

_____ Call the Poison Control Center and take the container.

_____ If a child may have swallowed something poisonous, do something.

_____ Make sure the emergency numbers are near the phone for the next emergency.

5. Write answers to the questions. Use complete sentences. (5 points)

1. Would you like to live in the mountains? Why or why not?

    _____

    _____

2. What are some advantages of a healthy diet?

    _____

    _____

3. Do you believe that the people of Hunza, the Caucasus, and Vilcabamba live so long? Why or why not?

    _____

    _____

4. What do you suggest for a long and healthy life?

    _____

    _____

5. What medical problem do you think scientists and researchers should try to solve?

    _____

    _____

Name _____   **Date** _____

1. Match each word with its meaning. (5 points)

___	1. behavior	a.	a center of attention or interest
___	2. concentration	b.	feeling hopeful and happy about something
___	3. reactions	c.	not feeling content or happy about something
___	4. tension	d.	giving close attention to something
___	5. focus	e.	feeling excited or worried because of a
___	6. beneficial		strange situation
___	7. dissatisfied	f.	a response to something
___	8. envious	g.	mental or nervous pressure
___	9. suspenseful	h.	feeling unhappy because another person has
___	10. optimistic		something you want
		i.	the actions or conduct of a person
		j.	helpful

2. Write *T* for true statements and *F* for false statements. (5 points)

___ 1. Television and the other visual media are never helpful to people.

___ 2. In families that watch a lot of television, there may be little communication between the family members.

___ 3. Watching a lot of television can help a person think better and be more logical.

___ 4. The violence on television may give people bad dreams.

___ 5. Some people believe that television is more real, so normal life seems boring to them.

3. Circle the letter of the correct word. (5 points)

1. I cannot _____ with the radio on. Please turn it off.

   a. concentrate   b. concentration   c. concentrated

2. I really don't like to watch _____ movies.

   a. suspense   b. suspend   c. suspenseful

3. We were all _____ with the ending of the movie.

   a. dissatisfaction   b. dissatisfy   c. dissatisfied

4. The crowd watched with great _____ the last minutes of the match.

   a. excitment   b. excite   c. exciting

5. I didn't _____ that we had a test today.

    a. realism   b. realize   c. real

4. Write the entertainment category you would use to find things to do. Use the choices from the box. (5 points)

live theater	TV programming	radio
recitals/concerts	neighborhood movies	clubs

1. I want to watch my favorite soap opera and the local news show. _____

2. I want to see a play acted out by people on stage. _____

3. I want to watch a new film with some friends. _____

4. I want to listen to an orchestra perform music by Mozart and Handel. _____

5. I want to go out with some friends to listen to a small band, dance, and have something to eat.

    _____

5. Write answers to the questions. Use complete sentences. (5 points)

1. How often do you watch TV?

    _____

    _____

2. Why do you watch (or don't watch) TV?

    _____

    _____

3. What kind of TV programs and movies do you enjoy?

    _____

    _____

4. Do you think that TV shows and movies are too violent? Why?

    _____

    _____

5. What do you think should be changed to improve TV shows?

    _____

    _____

Name _____   **Date** _____

1. Match each word with its meaning. (5 points)

   ____ 1. mate   a. having an unfriendly behavior

   ____ 2. interview   b. features or qualities of a person

   ____ 3. examine   c. note hopeful or confident

   ____ 4. reply   d. to look at or study carefully

   ____ 5. potential   e. to complete or write in information

   ____ 6. aggressive   f. to talk to face-to-face; to have a conversation with

   ____ 7. characteristics   g. partner; companion

   ____ 8. optimistic   h. hopeful; expecting the best

   ____ 9. fill out   i. possible

   ____ 10. discouraged   j. to say an answer

2. Write *T* for true statements and *F* for false statements. (5 points)

   ____ 1. In arranged marriages, parents choose who their children will marry.

   ____ 2. People can search for partners on the Web.

   ____ 3. You can meet people with similar interests in special interest clubs.

   ____ 4. In computer dating, a person matches you with someone of similar interests.

   ____ 5. People place personal ads in newspapers in video-dating clubs.

3. Circle the letter of the correct word. (5 points)

1. We are going to the bookstore after class. Do you want to go _____, too?

    a. there   b. it   c. them

2. Were Bill and Julie in class this morning? I didn't see _____.

    a. him   b. us   c. them

3. Why do many women join sports clubs? Because _____ like to exercise and meet people with similar interests.

    a. they   b. them   c. there

4. We are making a video as a class project. _____ sounds like fun!

    a. We   b. That   c. They

5. Sara filled out an application. Then she sent _____ to the dating service.

    a. it   b. her   c. them

4. Write *F* for statements that are facts and *0* for statements that are opinions. (5 points)

    ___ 1. A computer dating service is the best way to meet people.

    ___ 2. Some people are unfriendly or aggressive in dance clubs.

    ___ 3. A health club is a good place to meet someone who enjoys sports and exercise.

    ___ 4. Dating by video is the worst way to meet people.

    ___ 5. The perfect mate should be someone who has the same job or profession as you.

5. Write answers to the questions. Use complete sentences. (5 points)

    1. Where do (did) you meet your friends?

    _____

    _____

    2. How do (did) you meet your friends?

    _____

    _____

    3. What characteristics are important in a boyfriend or girlfriend?

    _____

    _____

    4. Do you talk to other people on the Web? Why or why not?

    _____

    _____

    5. What do you think is the best way to meet the "perfect mate"?

    _____

    _____

Name _____   **Date** _____

1. Match each word with its meaning. (5 points)

___ 1. invitation

___ 2. hospitality

___ 3. appreciation

___ 4. etiquette

___ 5. advise

___ 6. grateful

___ 7. appropriate

___ 8. considerate

___ 9. celebrate

___ 10. elaborate

a. thoughtfulness

b. to observe an occasion with special festivities

c. a spoken or written way of asking a person to do something

d. to recommend or suggest

e. complex; having many details

f. kind treatment of guests

g. rules of behavior

h. thankful

i. proper; suitable

j. thoughtful; thinking of others' feelings

2. Write *T* for true statements and *F* for false statements. (5 points)

___ 1. Customs for dinner parties are the same around the world.

___ 2. In nearly all cultures, it's a nice idea to bring a gift to the host of a party.

___ 3. Before eating at a dinner party, guests often talk and have some snacks.

___ 4. If you are the host of a party, you should spend all your time in the kitchen preparing the food.

___ 5. A host doesn't want his or her guests to be comfortable.

3. Circle the letter of the correct word. (5 points)

1. Long ago, the Celts _____ to make big fires to frighten ghosts.

   a. use   b. used   c. using

2. Later, the Christians _____ a holiday on November 1.

   a. had   b. has   c. having

3. Hundreds of years ago, people _____ that witches could tell the future.

   a. believing   b. believes   c. believed

4. Today, children _____ to homes in disguise for Halloween.

   a. went   b. go   c. gone

5. In Latin American cultures, people _____ their relatives who have died.

    a. remember   b. remembering   c. remembers

4. Write the type of card you would use for the special occasions. Use the choices from the box. (5 points)

anniversary card	party invitation	wedding announcement
get-well card	sympathy card	thank-you note

1. What should I sent to my sick friend? _____

2. What should I send to my friends and relatives when I get married? _____

3. What should I send to a host to show I am grateful? _____

4. What should I sent to ask my friends to a party? _____

5. What should I when a relative of my friend has died? _____

5. Write answers to the questions. Use complete sentences. (5 points)

1. Do you like to give parties?

    _____
    _____

2. What kinds of parties do you like to go to?

    _____
    _____

3. What does a good guest do at a party?

    _____
    _____

4. What does a good host do?

    _____
    _____

5. What is a holiday or celebration that you like? Why do you like it?

    _____
    _____

Name _____   **Date** _____

1. Match each word with its meaning. (5 points)

___	1. radiation	a.	causing argument or debate
___	2. treatments	b.	to enter by force or to spread harm through
___	3. distribute	c.	involving advanced scientific devices and machines
___	4. controversial		
___	5. interactive	d.	the act of getting in the way of something
___	6. high-tech	e.	ways of giving medical care
___	7. automatically	f.	watching over and keeping track of
___	8. monitoring	g.	to give out; to supply
___	9. interference	h.	nuclear energy; waves of light and energy
___	10. invade	i.	relating to a computer program in which a person and computer act on or affect each other
		j.	in a manner that is self-operating

2. Write *T* for true statements and *F* for false statements. (5 points)

___ 1. Everyone agrees that technology is always good.

___ 2. E-mail is an electronic way to write letters.

___ 3. Most families in the U.S. have many appliances and machines that use computer technology.

___ 4. Some examples of computer technology in the medical sciences are sensors, CAT scans, and laser surgery.

___ 5. Computers and television are going to improve relationships between people.

3. Circle the letter of the correct word. (5 points)

1. Computer information _____ help save patients.

   a. can   b. is   c. are

2. Computers _____ made it possible to run a home electronically.

   a. have   b. are   c. will

3. You _____ set the washing machine to go on at a certain time.

   a. has   b. are   c. can

4. People wonder if technology_____ improve the health and happiness of humans.

    a. will   b. is   c. has

5. Science _____ continue to move forward.

    a. is   b. will   c. do

4. VCR Instructions: Number the following statements in the proper order. (5 points)

_____ Turn off the TV and VCR when you are finished.

_____ Insert a video cassette.

_____ Press the PLAY button.

_____ Turn on the TV and set the VCR channel.

_____ Use the Tracking Control to adjust the picture or sound.

5. Write answers to the questions. Use complete sentences. (5 points)

1. Do you use computers? How?

_____

_____

2. What electronic or computer appliances do you use at home, school, or work?

_____

_____

3. Do you think computers and technology make life better?

_____

_____

4. Should scientists continue to invent new technology? Why or why not?

_____

_____

5. What problems and questions are there about computers and technology?

_____

_____

Name _____   **Date** _____

1. Match each word with its meaning. (5 points)

___ 1. consumer

___ 2. brand

___ 3. misinformation

___ 4. motive

___ 5. admit

___ 6. unpopular

___ 7. advertise

___ 8. generic

___ 9. defective

___ 10. misleading

a. describing a whole class of products

b. something that makes a person act in a certain way

c. a person that buys or uses something

d. a particular kind or make of an item

e. false or incomplete information

f. not perfect; having a mistake

g. to confess that something is true

h. wrong or false information

i. to call attention to a product

j. not well liked

2. Write *T* for true statements and *F* for false statements. (5 points)

___ 1. Commercials and ads tell people all the important facts about products.

___ 2. Advertisers want people to know the disadvantages of their products.

___ 3. Advertisers use different ads for different groups of people.

___ 4. People buy products in packages of certain colors.

___ 5. People like words like "new," "improved," and "natural."

3. Circle the letter of the correct word. (5 points)

1. Advertisers want _____ you buy their products.

   a. to see   b. see   c. seeing

2. Advertisers ask psychologists _____ people's choices.

   a. to study   b. study   c. studying

3. _____ leads us to buy things.

   a. To advertise   b. Advertise   c. Advertising

4. Fear is a reason for _____ a product.

   a. to buy   b. buy   c. buying

5. I like _____ that advertising doesn't affect me.

   a. thinking   b. think   c. to think

4. Write what you should read or use to be a good consumer. Use the choices from the box. (5 points)

list of ingredients	newspaper ads	small print
generic items	discount stores	consumer laws

1. What do I check to see what is on sale at a store? _____

2. Where do I look to see what materials are used to make an item? _____

3. Where can I shop and save money on lower priced items? _____

4. Where should I look at for questions about false and misleading ads? _____

5. Where can I check to see if an advertiser is trying to hide some misinformation?

   _____

5. Write answers to the questions. Use complete sentences. (5 points)

1. Where do you like to shop?

   _____

   _____

2. How do you decide what to buy?

   _____

   _____

3. Do you like to buy famous brands or generic brands? Why?

   _____

   _____

4. What is an ad that you like?

   _____

   _____

5. Have you had any problems with misleading or false advertising?

   _____

   _____

Placement Test Answer Key

Part 1 Determining Meaning and Usage from Context

Example: d

1. b
2. d
3. a
4. c
5. d
6. a
7. d
8. a
9. a
10. c

Part 2 Idiomatic Expressions

Example: a

1. c
2. b
3. d
4. c
5. c

Part 3 Scanning for Members of Word Families

Example: b

1. a
2. b
3. d
4. c
5. b

Part 4 Reading Comprehension

Reading 1
Example: F

1. F
2. T
3. F
4. F
5. F

Reading 2
Example: F

1. F
2. T
3. F
4. T
5. F

Reading 3
Example: b

1. c
2. c
3. d
4. c
5. b
6. c
7. c
8. a
9. d
10. c

Reading 4
Example: a

1. b
2. c
3. a
4. d
5. a
6. c
7. d
8. c
9. c
10. d

Answer Keys for Chapter Quizzes

Chapter 1

1.
1. d
2. g
3. a
4. h
5. c
6. j
7. i
8. e
9. b
10. f

2.
1. F
2. F
3. T
4. T
5. F

3.
1. b
2. a
3. b
4. b
5. a

4.
1. Gymnasium
2. Admissions and Records
3. Computer Center
4. Bookstore
5. Financial Aid Office

5. Answers will vary.

Chapter 2

1.
1. e
2. c
3. i
4. f
5. a
6. d
7. j
8. b
9. h
10. g

2.
1. F
2. T
3. F
4. F
5. T

3.
1. b
2. c
3. b
4. a
5. a

4.
1. storms
2. oceans
3. weather
4. continents
5. climate

5. Answers will vary.

Chapter 3

1.
1. e
2. c
3. g
4. i
5. d
6. b
7. a
8. j
9. f
10. h

2.
1. T
2. F
3. F
4. T
5. F

3.
1. b
2. c
3. a
4. c
5. a

4.
1. high protein foods
2. nutrients
3. junk foods
4. convenience foods
5. natural foods

5. Answers will vary.

Chapter 4

1.
1. f
2. d
3. h
4. b
5. i
6. c
7. j
8. a
9. e
10. g

2.
1. F
2. T
3. T
4. F
5. T

3.
1. b
2. a
3. a
4. c
5. b

4.
1. Department of Motor Vehicles
2. Libraries
3. Legal Services
4. Community College
5. Housing

5. Answers will vary.

Chapter 5

1.
1. e
2. h
3. f
4. j
5. a
6. d
7. b
8. i
9. g
10. c

2.
1. F
2. T
3. T
4. F

5. T

3.
1. c
2. a
3. c
4. b
5. b

4.
1. marriage
2. customary
3. universal
4. common
5. modernization

5. Answers will vary.

Chapter 6

1.
1. j
2. a
3. i
4. b
5. h
6. c
7. g
8. d
9. f
10. e

2.
1. T
2. F
3. F
4. T
5. F

3.
1. c
2. c
3. a
4. b
5. c

4.
1. Lectures
2. Literary Readings
3. Music
4. Art and Architecture
5. Cultural Festivals

5. Answers will vary.

Chapter 7

1.
1. g
2. d
3. i
4. f
5. j
6. b
7. e
8. a
9. b
10. h

2.
1. T
2. F
3. F
4. T
5. F

3.
1. b
2. a
3. c
4. a
5. c

4. 3, 4, 2, 1, 5

5. Answers will vary.

Chapter 8

1.
1. i
2. d
3. f
4. g
5. a
6. j
7. c
8. h
9. e
10. b

2.
1. F
2. T
3. F
4. T
5. T

3.
1. a
2. c
3. c

4. a
5. b

4.
1. TV programming
2. Live theater
3. Neighborhood movies
4. Recitals/concerts
5. Clubs

5. Answers will vary.

Chapter 9

1.
1. g
2. f
3. d
4. j
5. i
6. a
7. b
8. h
9. e
10. c

2.
1. T
2. T
3. T
4. F
5. F

3.
1. a
2. c
3. a
4. b
5. a

4.
1. O
2. F
3. F
4. O
5. O

5. Answers will vary.

Chapter 10

1.
1. c
2. f
3. a
4. g
5. d

6. h
7. i
8. j
9. b
10. e

2.
1. F
2. T
3. T
4. F
5. F

3.
1. b
2. a
3. c
4. b
5. a

4.
1. get-well card
2. wedding announcement
3. thank-you card
4. party invitation
5. sympathy card

5. Answers will vary.

Chapter 11

1.
1. h
2. e
3. g
4. a
5. i
6. c
7. j
8. f
9. d
10. b

2.
1. F
2 T
3. T
4. T
5. F

3.
1. a
2. a
3. c
4. a
5. b

4. 5, 2, 3, 1, 4

5. Answers will vary.

Chapter 12

1.
1. c
2. d
3. h
4. b
5. g
6. j
7. i
8. a
9. f
10. e

2.
1. F
2. F
3. F
4. T
5. T

3.
1. a
2. a
3. c
4. a
5. c

4.
1. newspaper ads
2. list of ingredients
3. discount stores
4. consumer laws
5. small print

5. Answers will vary.